AVIATION

AV-8B Harrier II

The US Marine Corps' VSTOL Jet Aircraft

KEN NEUBECK

SCHIFFER MILITARY
4880 Lower Valley Road Atglen, PA 19310

Library of Congress Control Number: 2021942420

Designed by Justin Watkinson
Type set in Impact/Minion Pro/Univers LT Std

ISBN: 978-0-7643-6340-5
Printed in India

Published by Schiffer Publishing, Ltd.
4880 Lower Valley Road
Atglen, PA 19310
Phone: (610) 593-1777; Fax: (610) 593-2002
Email: Info@schifferbooks.com
www.schifferbooks.com

Acknowledgments

The author acknowledges the help of a number of sources in this book, including Dave Ashley, John Gourley, Dennis R. Jenkins, Pima Air and Space Museum staff members, Lauren Hohl, James Stemm, and Chuck Stump. In addition, other organizations provided photos, such as the Long Island Republic Airport Historical Society (LIRAHS), NASA, the RAF Air Historical Branch, the US Navy, the US Marines, and the US Air Force.

Contents

CHAPTER 1	Early VSTOL Aircraft Concepts	004
CHAPTER 2	Origins of the Harrier Jump Jet	014
CHAPTER 3	USMC History with the AV-8A and AV-8C Harriers	024
CHAPTER 4	AV-8B Development	035
CHAPTER 5	UK Second-Generation Harriers	047
CHAPTER 6	USMC Harrier Details	050
CHAPTER 7	USMC Squadrons	073
CHAPTER 8	USMC AV-8B Combat Operations	086
CHAPTER 9	Foreign Harriers	104
CHAPTER 10	Legacy of the Harrier Jump Jet	110

CHAPTER 1

Early VSTOL Aircraft Concepts

In this artist concept of a design study for a VSTOL aircraft by Grumman, known as the G-698 program, for the US Navy, there are rotating engines positioned under each wing. It was envisioned at the time that this aircraft would take off from different US Navy ships besides the US Navy aircraft carrier as seen in this drawing. *Grumman archives via LIRAHS*

Vertical/short takeoff and landing (VSTOL) is a concept that has been drawing the attention of many companies and military organizations, both in the US and Europe, since the 1950s. The VSTOL concept has captured the imagination because it solves a number of problem associated with conventional aircraft in the area of restricted landing space, both in challenging terrains and on naval ships.

During the 1960s, many of the major US aerospace companies conducted various feasibility and trade studies on VSTOL designs both for the US Air Force and the US Navy. Indeed, to adequately cover the complete scope of these efforts in the US and Europe would cover several volumes of material.

The concept of VSTOL was considered because of situations that arise during operating in certain locations where conventional landing fields for aircraft are not possible. In addition, the concept of using a VSTOL aircraft allows for enhanced capability for US Navy ships, not only for conventional aircraft carriers but for other US Navy ships that can carry and dispatch helicopters.

The great majority of these studies were paper design and rarely reached the stage of a full-scale mockup. The efforts of these companies involved in the early studies show that the collective thinking was similar in regard to VSTOL concepts. Indeed, these concepts include the idea of having pivoting engine exhaust that could provide downward thrust during vertical takeoff and forward thrust for regular flight.

There were many challenges regarding VSTOL technology. The engine had to have the ability to rotate or have its exhaust portion rotate to provide the thrust. It was necessary to have a design that would have smooth transition from vertical flight into forward flight. Finally, some aerodynamic issues such as downwash, not known previously, had to be understood and addressed.

VSTOL concepts under consideration were in two basic directions—those for aircraft designs and those for helicopter designs. The latter concept would be developed by Bell/Boeing for the XV-15 prototype and ultimately the V-22 Osprey, which is operated by the US Marines (MV-22) and the US Air Force (CV-22).

For insight on the VSTOL design history, some of the early VSTOL design concepts are provided here, and it can be seen how they strongly resemble the eventual Harrier VSTOL concept, even though few of these concepts resulted in a production aircraft program.

Some of the design studies resulted in the actual building of prototype and flight test aircraft. For example, the Republic Aviation Corporation was involved in directing the flight testing of an early VSTOL aircraft that was built: the Ryan Aeronautical XV-5A aircraft for the US Army. The XV-5A began flight testing at Edwards AFB in California in 1964, extending into the 1970s, but no further contracts developed.

Additional artist concepts of the Grumman G-698 VSTOL concept study for a US Navy aircraft that resembles a S-3 Viking show the transition from using vertical takeoff from the ground to forward movement in flight. The transition is accomplished through the use of two rotating engine nacelle assemblies that pivot under the wings. A full-scale mockup was constructed for the program that underwent wind tunnel testing at NASA before the program ended. *Grumman Archives via LIRAHS*

During the 1960s, McDonnell came up with a VSTOL concept that was somewhat similar to the Grumman G-698 with the McAir VSTOL aircraft for the US Navy, shown here. This aircraft would have rotatable engines under each wing as well, with a unique tail section. No actual mockups appear to have been built. *NASA*

In addition to the design shown above, McDonnell came up with another concept for a US Navy fighter that was VSTOL. This design featured the rotatable engines located above the wing. *NASA*

An artist concept of a design study for a potential VSTOL aircraft that was conducted by Fairchild Hiller for the US Air Force, showing both VSTOL and forward flight. This design concept has the two engines embedded in the lower fuselage, with variable-direction thrust exhaust. *Fairchild Republic Archives via LIRAHS*

Another artist concept of a 1960s design study for a potential VSTOL design by Fairchild Republic for the US Air Force, showing a different concept in which three turbofans are located behind the cockpit. *Fairchild Republic Archives via LIRAHS*

Another artist concept of a design study in 1966 for a VSTOL by Fairchild Republic for a joint US Air Force and German air force by EWR/Fairchild International (a combination of Entwicklungsring Sud. and the Republic Aviation Division of Fairchild Industries). The concept shows a rotating thrust exhaust located underneath the engine inlets. *Fairchild Republic Archives via LIRAHS*

Artist concept of the EWR/Fairchild VSTOL design shows the aircraft flying in vertical mode through the downward thrust created by the exhaust of the engines rotated and positioned downward. There was a seven-month design study for this concept, but no formal prototype was built, and the program ended in 1969. *Fairchild Republic Archives via LIRAHS*

Another program was a joint venture between Ryan Aeronautic and Fairchild Republic for a VSTOL aircraft known as the XV-5 Vertifan. There were two XV-5A aircraft built. The first was destroyed in a crash during a public flight demonstration on April 27, 1965, killing Ryan test pilot Lou Everett. The second aircraft was extensively damaged on October 5, 1966, during trials as a rescue aircraft, when a suspended "horse collar" survivor sling was ingested into a wing fan. The pilot, Maj. David H. Tittle, was fatally injured as a result of the ejection seat propelling him out of the craft after it had hit the concrete airport surface. *Fairchild Republic Archives via LIRAHS*

The XV-5A was piloted by one pilot. After the crash of the first aircraft, the remaining XV-5A aircraft that is shown here would be repaired and rebuilt as the modified XV-5B, with flight testing continuing until 1971. An XV-5B can be seen on display at the United States Army Aviation Museum, Fort Rucker, Alabama. *Fairchild Republic Archives via LIRAHS*

The XV-5A Vertifan aircraft was powered by two General Electric J85-GE-5 turbojets with 2,658 lbs. of thrust. General Electric X353-5 lift fans were in the wings, and a smaller fan was in the nose. These were powered by engine exhaust gas, used for vertical takeoff and landing (VTOL). The lift fan in each wing had a hinged cover on the upper wing surface, which was opened for VTOL. A set of louvered vanes underneath each of the wing fans could vector the thrust fore and aft and provided yaw control, with engine power settings determining the lift from the fans. *Fairchild Republic Archives via LIRAHS*

Another concept for VSTOL design was the Ling Temco XC-142A, which was built by Vought. The design incorporated the rotation of the entire wing, with the four engines for vertical flight. This concept was planned for the triservice assault program (US Navy, USAF, and US Army), and a total of five test aircraft were built. The plan was to use it as a troop carrier for carrying thirty-two troops. The first conventional flight took place in September 1964, and the first VSTOL and transition flight took place in January 1965. *NASA*

The radical design concept of the XC-142A saw several issues during flight testing, including vibration and noise issues, along with the wing flexing. A number of hard landings were experienced as well. The remaining aircraft was turned over to NASA, which tested the aircraft from May 1966 through 1970. This aircraft is now preserved at the National Museum of the US Air Force in Dayton, Ohio. *USAF*

The US Marine Corps has been involved significantly in the field of VSTOL aircraft. The V-22 tilt-rotor Osprey made by Bell and Boeing has been a major effort, with the first flight made in 1989. Pictured here is the third prototype V-22 aircraft, which is on display at the American Helicopter Museum in West Chester, Pennsylvania. The rotors rotate on the ends of the wing structure. *Ken Neubeck*

There were tremendous growing pains during the development of the V-22 program, in which a number of crashes resulting in fatalities were experienced during the early stages of the program. The complexity of the aircraft, along with new phenomena being encountered, led to a long development process. Pictured here is MV-22 from US Marine Corps Squadron VMM-162 during a visit at Republic Airport in Long Island, New York, in 2019. *Ken Neubeck*

There was a unique UAV that incorporated the VSTOL concept that the US Coast Guard had in the form of the Bell Eagle Eye Vertical Unmanned Vehicle (VUAV), which was developed in 1993. The aircraft made use of the tilt-motor technology used in the V-22 design. Shown here is one of the two ⅞-scale demonstrator aircraft that were built by Bell. *US Coast Guard*

A full-scale flight test model was built by Bell for further testing until the program was put on hold in 2002. The program was not able to get any further interest from the US Navy or from European countries. One of the ⅞ demonstrators is on display at the Patuxent River Naval Air Museum, Maryland. Note that the rotors rotate at the end of the wings like the V-22 Osprey. *Ken Neubeck*

CHAPTER 2

Origins of the Harrier Jump Jet

The key to successful VSTOL efforts for the Harrier jump jet led to the development of the Rolls-Royce Pegasus engine (seen here on display in RAF Hendon Museum). The transition aspect of the VSTOL concept was accomplished when the Pegasus engine had the ability to redirect thrust internally for forward flight and for VSTOL flight, through the rear exhaust section, as shown on the left. Hydraulic and fuel system components are located on the top of the engine. *John Gourley*

Going from a paper design concept to an actual working VSTOL aircraft required many steps, and it began when engineers Stanley Hooker from the Bristol Engine Company, along with Ralph Hooper and Sydney Camm, both of the Hawker Aircraft company, worked on a directable-fan-jet design for aircraft in 1957. The engine that was developed for this was designated as Pegasus.

At the same time, the Hawker Company was working on a replacement aircraft for the Hawker Hunter that would be initially designated as the P.1121, eventually replaced by the P.1127, in conjunction with NATO. The development occurred during a time of defense-funding uncertainty in the UK, but eventually, two P.1127 prototypes would be authorized to be built in 1959. These prototypes were designated as XP831 and XP836.

After construction of the two prototypes, extensive developmental testing on the airframe and the engine occurred, beginning in 1960 in Dunsfold in the UK. A critical step that was eventually achieved was the smooth transition from vertical-takeoff mode into regular flight mode. The first flight took place in October 1960.

The UK Minister of Supply ordered another four prototypes in 1960. The Pegasus engine went through design improvements to go from the initial 11,300 pounds of thrust to 15,000 pounds of thrust. It was the last prototype (XP984) that introduced the swept-wing design concept. The first three prototypes would eventually crash during testing.

In 1962, three countries—the UK, the United States, and Germany—collaborated in the funding of nine production-type aircraft that would be designated as the Kestrel FGA.1. By this time, the Pegasus 5 engine, with 15,000 pounds of thrust, was available to be incorporated into these aircraft. Evaluation of these aircraft would be finalized by November 1965. Eventually, Germany would drop out of the program.

By 1965, six of the FGA.1 aircraft were transferred to the US (with the other three staying in the UK) for evaluation by the different services (US Air Force, Army, and Navy) and the aircraft was redesignated as the XV-6A, Testing occurred at Pax (Patuxent) River in Maryland and at Edwards AFB in California. Eventually, two of these aircraft would be assigned to NASA for testing. Around this point, the nickname "jump jet" was coined for this aircraft.

In response to NATO's request for VSTOL aircraft in 1961, Hawker began new work to initially replace the original P.1127 design, but requirement changes would bring it back to the original P.1127 design concept. Six preproduction aircraft were ordered by the RAF, with a follow-on order of sixty production aircraft that the RAF designated as GR.1. This version was fitted with a Pegasus 6 engine with 19,000 pounds of thrust. The first flight took place in 1967.

An interesting event involving the Harrier took place when the *Daily Mail* transatlantic air race between London and New York took place in May 1969 to commemorate the fiftieth anniversary of the first transatlantic crossing by John Adcock and Arthur Brown. Participants in this event included a RAF GR.1 Harrier that was flown by Tony Leky-Thompson, who lifted up off a coal yard in London to eventually land on a platform in a basin in New York City. The flight was a record six hours and eleven minutes and relied on aerial refueling over the Atlantic.

Kestrel #2 (USAF serial number 64-18262) is seen here as an outdoor display at the National Museum of the Air Force at Wright-Patterson AFB in Dayton, Ohio. The aircraft was the first one to be transported by the C-5A transport when it was moved from Edwards AFB in California to the museum in Ohio in 1970. *J. W. Hawkins collection via John Gourley*

Eventually a GR.3 version was developed with a Pegasus 11 engine that provided 21,500 pounds of thrust and would prove to be a definitive version of the Harrier for the RAF. Also, during the 1970s the FRS.1 Sea Harrier was developed for use by the Royal Navy (RN) on the Invincible-class aircraft carriers. Both the FRS.1 Sea Harrier and the GR.3 Harrier would be the first Harriers that would see combat action, when the aircraft participated in the 1982 Falklands War for the UK, where the aircraft proved its versatility and effectiveness. The Sea Harriers were the first Harrier to see action, beginning on May 1, 1982, with No. 800 Squadron attacking Argentine aircraft on the airfield at Port Stanley.

The Harrier was effective in close air support and in dogfights as well, in which the 30 mm cannon and the sidewinder missiles were key weapons used by Royal Navy Squadrons 800 and 801 in shooting down Argentine A-4s, Pucara, Daggar A, SA.300L, A-109A, B-26, and C-130 aircraft during the war. In addition to the aircraft that were destroyed, Sea Harriers would also put three Argentine ships out of action.

The Sea Harriers would fly 2,376 sorties, totaling 2,675 flight hours. The 1.1-hour duration per sortie is an indication of how close the Harriers were located to targets. Of the six Sea Harriers lost in the war, only two were due to actual combat action. The Harriers were a major weapon in this war.

The 30 mm Aden cannon pod used on the GR.3 Harrier was key to its success; however, a planned upgrade was the Aden-25 pod, which would use lighter 25 mm shells that could travel faster. This gun was proposed for use on the GR5 and GR7 Harrier models, but several developmental problems would ensue and the Aden-25 program was canceled in 1999. Both the GR5 and GR7 models were without gun pod capability and carried bombs and missiles only on the pylons. The lack of a gun pod would severely limit the effectiveness of the UK Harriers for the close-air-support role in future combat activity.

Eventually a GR.3 version was developed with a Pegasus 11 engine that provided 21,500 pounds of thrust, and this version would also be the baseline that would be used for the US Marine Corps (USMC) AV-8A versions of the Harrier (covered in the next chapter).

Kestrel #6 (serial number 64-18266) is seen here landing on USS *Raleigh* LPD in May 1966. Three branches of the US armed services, the Army, the Air Force and the Navy, all were involved in conducting tests on the Kestrel aircraft that were imported from the UK. *US Navy*

Kestrel #4 (serial number 64-18264) is positioned on a stand during electromagnetic field testing at Edwards AFB, California, in October 1967. The wingspan for the Kestrel aircraft is 22 feet, and at this stage of the program there are no hardpoints for weapon pylons added to the wings of the aircraft. *National Archives via Dennis R. Jenkins*

This is the center console for the XV-6A Kestrel. It contains the standard flight instruments, along with a unique instrument for an aircraft: the instantaneous vertical speed indicator (IVSI), which is located in the second row from the top. *National Archives via Dennis R. Jenkins*

For the XV-6A Kestrel, a cockpit simulator was built that was needed to train pilots for all unique aspects of flying the Kestrel, both for forward flight and vertical takeoff. *John Gourley*

After evaluation of the Kestrel aircraft by the US armed services, NASA was given two more to evaluate. Here is serial number 64-18266 in flight, which has been redesignated as NASA 521 at the Langley Research Center, Virginia, in 1968. The NASA emblem is on the vertical tail section. *NASA*

After completion of testing, surviving Kestrel XV-6A test aircraft were sent to museums for display, such as Kestrel #2 (serial number 64-18262), shown here at the USAF museum in Dayton, Ohio. *John Gourley*

Six preproduction Hawker Siddeley Harrier GR.1 aircraft are on display at the manufacturer's test facility at Dunsfold aerodrome, Surrey, UK, in 1968. The first RAF squadron to be equipped with the Harrier GR.1, RAF No. 1 Squadron, started to convert to the aircraft at RAF Wittering in April 1969. There would be sixty-nine examples of the GR.1 model, which were equipped with the Pegasus 6 engine. *RAF Air Historical Branch—open license*

GR.3 Harrier from RAF No. 1 Squadron lands in Port Stanley, Falkland Islands, in June 1982 during the conflict between the UK and Argentina. Ten GR.3 aircraft from this squadron participated in the war. *RAF Air Historical Branch—open license*

FRS.1 Sea Harrier from the UK's No. 800 Naval Air Squadron lands on USS *Eisenhower* in October 1984. This squadron was one of three FRS.1 squadrons that participated in the Falklands War in 1982, where it provided twelve of the twenty-eight FRS.1 aircraft that fought in the war. A total of six Sea Harriers were lost during the war. The Sea Harriers were a key weapons system for the Royal Navy in the war. *US Navy*

FR1.3 Sea Harrier (1,438 Sorties) and GR.3 Harrier (126 Sorties), Falkland War Combat Record				
Squadron	**No. A/C**	**A/C lost**	**Air-to-air kills**	**Air-to-ground kills**
800 (RN)	12	2	15	3
801 (RN)	8	4	8	1
809 (RN)	8	0	0	0
1 (RAF)	10	4	0	2
TOTALS	**38**	**10**	**23**	**6**

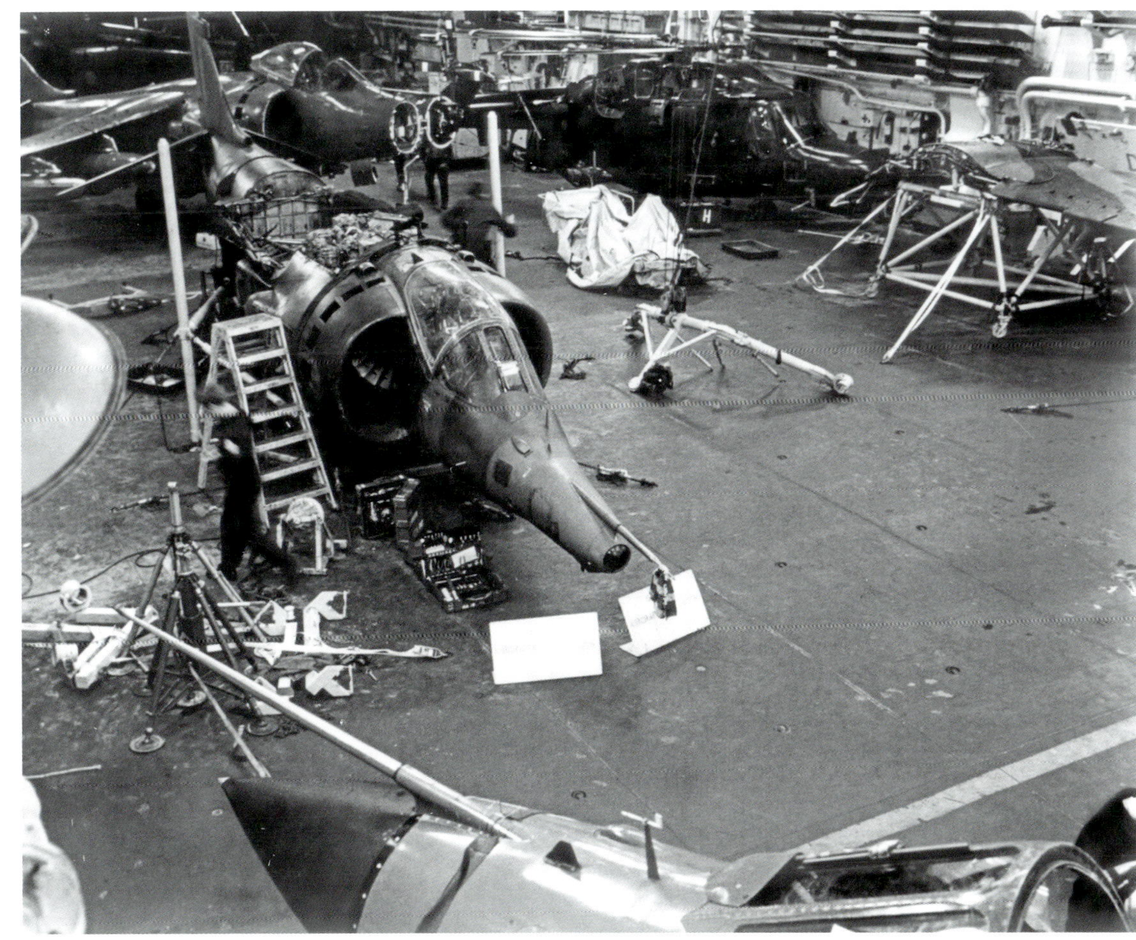

GR.3 Harrier from RAF No. 1 Squadron is being serviced inside the maintenance bay of HMS *Hermes.* In the foreground is the nose of a Royal Navy FRS.1 Sea Harrier. Both Harrier service types were serviced in the same area of the ship by maintenance personnel during the war. *RAF Air Historical Branch—open license*

Pictured here on the deck of HMS *Hermes* during combat operations during the 1982 Falklands War are both GR.3 Harriers (dark-colored aircraft with extended nose section) and FR.1 Sea Harriers (lighter-colored aircraft in front of helicopter) The two types of Harriers from the RAF and RN performed both in air-to-air combat and in the ground attack roles during the war, in which several Argentine targets were destroyed, including gun positions and even small intelligence ships. *RAF Air Historical Branch—open license*

Summary of First-Generation UK and US Harrier Models

Model	Quantity	Country	Engine	Thrust rating	First Flight
P.1127	10	UK	Pegasus 1	9,000 lbs.	1960
Kestrel FGA.1	3	UK	Pegasus 5	15,500 lbs.	1964
XV-6A (ex-Kestrel)	6	US	Pegasus 5	15,000 lbs.	1964
GR.1	61	UK	Pegasus 6	19,000 lbs.	1967
GR.1A	17	UK	Pegasus 10	20,500 lbs.	1967
GR.3	40	UK	Pegasus 11	21,500 lbs.	1969
AV-8A	102	US	Pegasus 11	21,500 lbs.	1970
AV-8C	47 (mod.)	US	Pegasus 11	21,500 lbs.	1979
FRS.1	57	UK	Pegasus 14	21,500 lbs.	1985
TAV-8A	8	US	Pegasus 11	21,500 lbs.	1970

GR1 Harrier of No. 1 Squadron is taking off from HMS *Ark Royal* during sea trials in May 1971. *RAF Air Historical Branch—open license*

CHAPTER 3

USMC History with the AV-8A and AV-8C Harriers

This is the first AV-8A Harrier that was delivered to the USMC, BuNo 158284, as it takes off from a US Navy amphibious assault ship in the early 1970s. This Harrier has tail code WF, which is the VMA-513 (Nightmares) Squadron. It is painted in a green-and-gray camouflage paint scheme, signifying its close-air-support role. *US Navy*

The AV-8A was the first version for the VSTOL mission by the USMC, and it would eventually end up being an iterative process for a suitable VSTOL aircraft design for the Marines. The design was initially based on the GR.1 Harrier, when the USMC showed interest in the aircraft around the time the first RAF Harrier squadron was established in 1969. This motivated Hawker Siddeley to further develop the aircraft in order to interest the USMC to buy a total of 102 aircraft. All the aircraft would be built at the Hawker Siddeley facility in the UK and then delivered to McDonnell Douglas in St. Louis, Missouri, for the company to fit the aircraft with US avionics and equipment prior to delivery to the US Marines.

The AV-8A entered service with the Marine Corps in 1971, replacing other aircraft such as the A-4 Skyhawk in the Marines' attack squadrons. These first-generation Harriers were handicapped in range and payload. In short-takeoff-and-landing configuration, the AV-8A carried less than half the 4,000-pound payload of the smaller A-4 Skyhawk, over a more limited radius.

Starting in 1979, the USMC began upgrading their AV-8As to the AV-8C configuration, since this upgrade would focus mainly on extending useful-service lives and improving VSTOL performance. A total of forty-seven AV-8A Harriers were converted to AV-8Cs. The AV-8C version included an upgraded radar.

The USMC used their Harriers primarily for close air support, operating from amphibious assault ships and, if needed, forward operating bases. Harrier squadrons saw several deployments overseas. The Harrier's ability to operate with minimal ground facilities and very short runways allowed it to be used at locations unavailable to other fixed-wing aircraft. The Harrier received criticism for having a high accident rate as well as a time-consuming maintenance process.

The AV-8C and the remaining AV-8A Harriers were completely retired by 1987, without this model seeing any combat action with the US. These were replaced by the Harrier II, designated as the AV-8B, which was introduced into service in 1985.

It became apparent that the Harrier was not a conventional aircraft to fly by any means, and it was tricky for pilots to learn how to maintain proper control to keep the aircraft level when in the hover mode. Thus, for such a unique aircraft, additional training was required for pilots. The AV-8A/C Harriers would experience several accidents during USMC use, with almost forty aircraft lost and some thirty pilots killed during the 1970s and 1980s.

AV-8A Harriers from VMA-513 are flying in a diamond format over their home USMC base at Yuma, Arizona, in 1975. This base is still active with AV-8 Harriers at the present time, over forty-five years later. *US Navy*

AV-8A Harrier BuNo 159255, from VMA-231, is dropping a Rockeye bomb over target range in 1979. The Harrier would be fitted with various weapons over the course of its service life. Its weapon capability has evolved into the inclusion of digital weapons. *US Navy*

AV-8A Harrier from VMA-513 is hovering over the flight deck of USS *Guam* in January 1972 while conducting operational testing over the Atlantic Ocean. USS *Guam* was the test bed for developing the concept of a ship carrying Harriers and helicopters, such as the SH-3 Sea King. It is noted that VSTOL capability of the Harrier would allow it to be assigned to US Navy amphibious assault ships in lieu of aircraft carrier. *US Navy*

A string of three AV-8A Harriers from VMA-513 are preparing for takeoff from USS *Belleau Wood*, an amphibious assault ship, in 1982. This ship would be eventually decommissioned in 2005 and sunk during target practice off Hawaii in 2006. *US Navy*

Two AV-8A Harriers from VMA-513 are next to a UH-1 Iroquois helicopter on USS *Nassau*, an amphibious assault ship, in April 1982. This ship would be later be decommissioned, in 2011. *US Navy*

The AV-8A VSTOL aircraft would be a very new concept for USMC pilots to learn, so a flight simulator with the cockpit was developed, which allowed the pilots to become familiar both with standard flight instruments and those instruments and controls associated with VSTOL features. The throttle nozzle quadrant was one unique feature and is seen here in its location on the left side of the cockpit. *John Gourley*

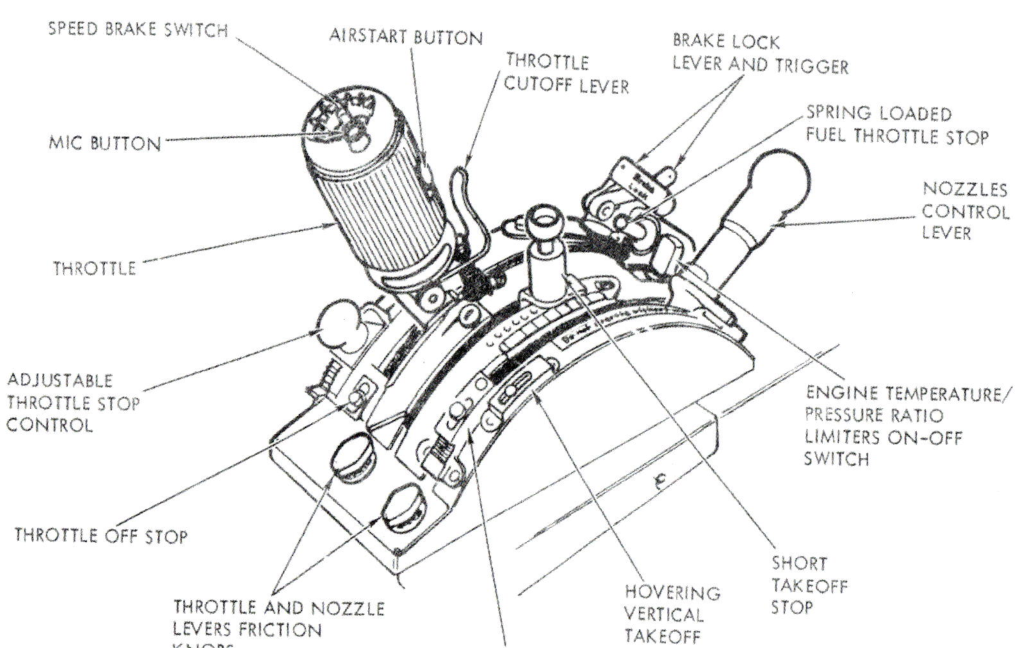

The different controls of the throttle nozzle quadrant are detailed in an illustration in the AV-8A flight control manual, as shown here.

Along with the initial order of AV-8A Harriers was an order of eight TAV-8A trainer aircraft. These aircraft would be assigned to VMAT-203 Squadron ("the Hawks"), which was based in Cherry Point, North Carolina. *USMC photo by Sgt. Cordova*

A TAV-8A Harrier from VMA-203 is landing during an air show. One of the TAV-8A (BuNo 159381) aircraft would be given to NASA for testing and is now on display in the Oakland Aviation Museum. *USMC photo by Sgt. T. K. Burch*

This is the YAV-8C development aircraft, BuNo 158384, which was on loan to McDonnell Douglas for flight testing in 1979. This aircraft would crash off the bow of USS *Tarawa* in the Pacific Ocean off the coast of Southern California in September 1980. *National Archives*

The YAV-8C development aircraft, BuNo 158384, is shown at the top of the photo, and below it is the YAV-8B development aircraft, BuNo 158394, on deck together during testing in 1983 to verify the AV-8C upgrade and the new AV-8B version. *National Archives*

This AV-8C, BuNo 158975, from VMA-513, is landing in Whiting Field in Florida in January 1982. It features a paint scheme using olive green and dark green. *US Navy*

AV-8C from VMA-513 is taking off from the deck of the US Navy's USS *Guadalcanal* in 1983. *US Navy*

This AV-8A Harrier, BuNo 159875, was retired and was installed as an outdoor display at the National Naval Aviation Museum in Pensacola, Florida. This photo was taken in 1993. *John Gourley*

At some point, AV-8A Harrier BuNo 158975 was moved from being an outdoor display to an indoor display. The aircraft is now hanging from the roof of the National Naval Aviation Museum for public viewing. *John Gourley*

This AV-8C Harrier, BuNo 159232, was converted from an AV-8A model and, after retirement from the USMC, is now on display at the USS *Intrepid* Air and Space Museum, in New York City. *Ken Neubeck*

This AV-8C model on display at the Intrepid Museum is painted in the dark-gray-and-olive-green camouflage scheme. It features the "Ace of Spades" emblem of VMA-231, which flew AV-8A models beginning in 1973. *Ken Neubeck*

This AV-8C Harrier, BuNo 158710, was on display at the Quonset Aviation Museum in Rhode Island prior to the museum closing in 2011. This display aircraft is outfitted with rocket launcher pods under each wing. *Ken Neubeck*

Close-up view of the AV-8C aircraft shows the unique refueling-probe structure that is fixed to the top of the left engine nacelle of the aircraft. Also, this model features an instrument probe that is located on the nose. *Ken Neubeck*

CHAPTER 4

AV-8B Development

Shown here is the second of four AV-8B prototypes (BuNo 161387) that was developed by McDonnell circa 1987. This aircraft was used for flight testing and is now on display at the Carolinas Aviation Museum, located in Charlotte, North Carolina. *McDonnell via John Gourley*

It became apparent that there were limitations to the AV-8A Harrier aircraft, particularly in the area of combat range and weapon payload capabilities. A joint effort between the US and the UK (between McDonnell Douglas and Hawker Siddeley) began in 1973, in which an advanced Harrier design was defined. This version was to be fitted with the Pegasus 15 engine.

However, a decrease in UK defense funding in 1975 prompted the withdrawal of the UK from this project, and the US elected not to continue. But in 1976, the US government authorized McDonnell Douglas to develop a substantially improved Harrier design without changing the existing engine. This would lead to two prototypes being converted in 1978 from existing AV-8A aircraft (BuNo 158394 and BuNo 158395) and redesignated as YAV-8B. The aircraft would feature new wings, new intakes, and new engine exhausts. The two prototypes first flew in November 1978 and February 1979, respectively.

There was pressure by the Department of Defense (DOD) and the US Navy to terminate the AV-8B program between 1978 and 1980 due to high costs and the pursuit of the F/A-18 Hornet aircraft to fill the ground support role. However, the program would still continue to be supported by the DOD at this time.

In August 1981, the UK came back into the program when British Aerospace (BAE) and McDonnell Douglas signed a mutual agreement. Work sharing was developed between the two companies, with production taking place in the McDonnell facility in St. Louis, Missouri.

In light of the success of the prototype program, AV-8B production commenced in 1981 with four full-scale-development (FSD) aircraft built, beginning with BuNo 161386, which had its first flight in November 1981. The next aircraft had a revision to the engine inlet and some changes to the wing structure, and this aircraft would first fly in 1983. First-production AV-8B Harriers were delivered to the USMC in December 1983. For the overall program, there was a total production of 162 AV-8B Harrier aircraft that would be built from 1983 through 1989. However, there would be two variants developed during the program.

The first variant was a night attack version that was developed during the AV-8B production run in 1987, and this was designated as AV-8B (NA). The eighty-seventh production Harrier aircraft would be modified to this version and was delivered in June 1987 for flight testing. The night attack version featured the addition of an infrared sensor located on top of the nose section, along with an updated cockpit.

A total of sixty-six AV-8Bs (NA) would be produced, with deliveries to the USMC beginning in September 1987. The RAF GR7 is the corresponding counterpart of the AV-8B (NA).

At this point in time, there were still difficulties with flying the Harrier. During the time period from January 1985 through December 1991, there were thirty-four class A mishaps (not counting Desert Storm losses) that resulted in eight fatalities. The AV-8B experienced more than two times as many class A mishaps per 100,000 flight hours as compared to other US Navy and US Air Force tactical aircraft during the same time period.

As a result, an audit was conducted by the Office of the Inspector General in July 1992, which identified the issues and recommended corrective action for better performance. This included more-thorough testing of engine upgrades, correcting airframe design issues, and improving training and operating procedures of pilots and maintainers.

An improved Harrier, the AV-8B Harrier II or Harrier Plus, was developed and would have additional radar and weapon capabilities. A prototype, BuNo 164129, was developed by modifying an existing AV-8B Harrier, and this would fly in June 1992. Conversion began at the end of 1994 and continued until 2003, with a total of seventy-two AV-8Bs remanufactured into this version. A total of 824 Harriers aircraft of all models have been built since the program began in 1969.

There are no new plans to procure any more AV-8B Harriers, and the plan is for the new F-35B aircraft to eventually take over the role of the AV-8B, although existing Harriers continue on until this occurs.

An assembly line was set up for AV-8B production at the McDonnell Douglas facility located in St. Louis, Missouri. Here an operator is using a special setup to drill holes into an AV-8B wing skin surface at the facility. *McDonnell via John Gourley*

Summary of Second-Generation UK and US Harrier Models

Model	Quantity	Country	Engine	Thrust rating	First flight
YA-8B	2 (mod.)	US	Pegasus 11	21,500 lbs.	1978
AV-8B	306	US	Pegasus 11-21	21,750 lbs.	1981
AV-8B+	31 (new)	US	Pegasus 11-61	23,800 lbs.	1993
GR5	41	UK	Pegasus 11	21,500 lbs.	1985
GR5A	19	UK	Pegasus 11-21	21,750 lbs.	1985
GR7	96	UK	Pegasus 11-61	23,800 lbs.	1990
GR7A	5	UK	Pegasus 11-61	23,800 lbs.	1990
GR9	20	UK	Pegasus 11-61	23,000 lbs.	2003
GR9A	50	UK	Pegasus 11-61	23,800 lbs.	2004
TAV-8B	28	US	Pegasus 11-61	23,800 lbs.	1981
T10	3	UK	Pegasus 11-61	23,800 lbs.	1981
T12	10	UK	Pegasus 11-61	23,800 lbs.	1981

The AV-8B has the option of conventional forward roll takeoff or taking off in VSTOL model. *Ken Neubeck*

With regard to understanding the maximum takeoff weight for the Harrier, it is important to understand that the aircraft can carry more weapon load when conducting a conventional rolling takeoff and landing, compared to carrying less load when conducting a VSTOL or vertical takeoff. *Ken Neubeck*

AV-8B Harrier II Plus Specifications	
Power plant	One Rolls-Royce Pegasus 11 -61 [F402-RE-408] Turbojet
Maximum speed	673 mph (Mach 0.9)
Service ceiling	50,000 feet
Range	1,400 miles
Empty weight	14,865 pounds

The AV-8B has been in USMC service since 1983 and is still in active USMC service. *Ken Neubeck*

The diagrams above are taken from the NAVTOPS manual and detail the differences between the two versions of the AV-8B, along with the two-seat TAV-8B trainer version.

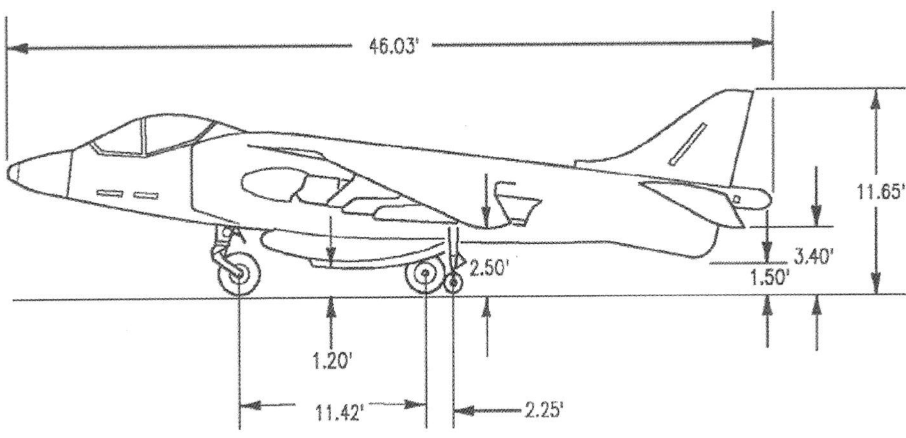

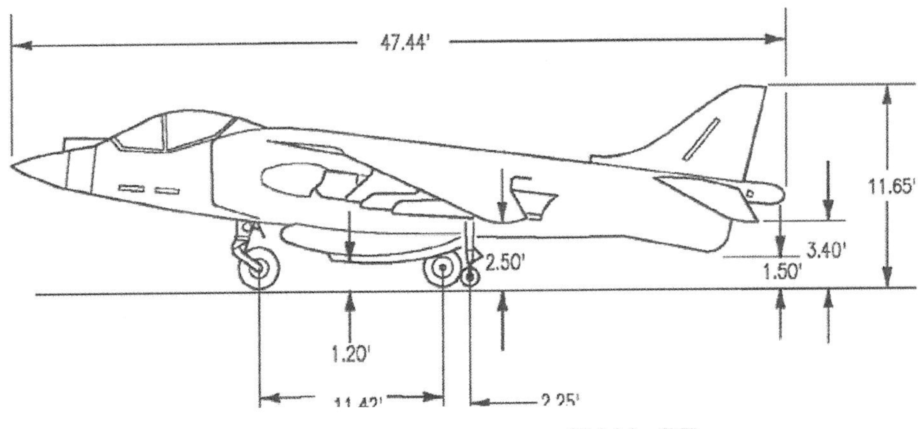

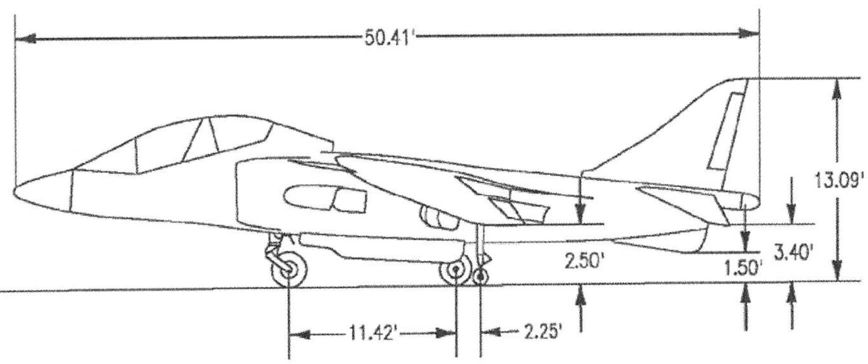

VMA-213 Squadron ("Ace of Spades") was one of the first USMC squadrons to receive the V-8B Harrier. Here is an early-production AV-8B for the USMC operating in the woods of Cherry Point, North Carolina, in March 1988. The aircraft is painted in camouflage colors of gray and olive green, typical of the scheme for close-air-support aircraft. *McDonnell via John Gourley*

The layout of the equipment for the two different versions of the AV-8B aircraft and the TAV-8B aircraft is shown above and is taken from the NAVTOPS manual.

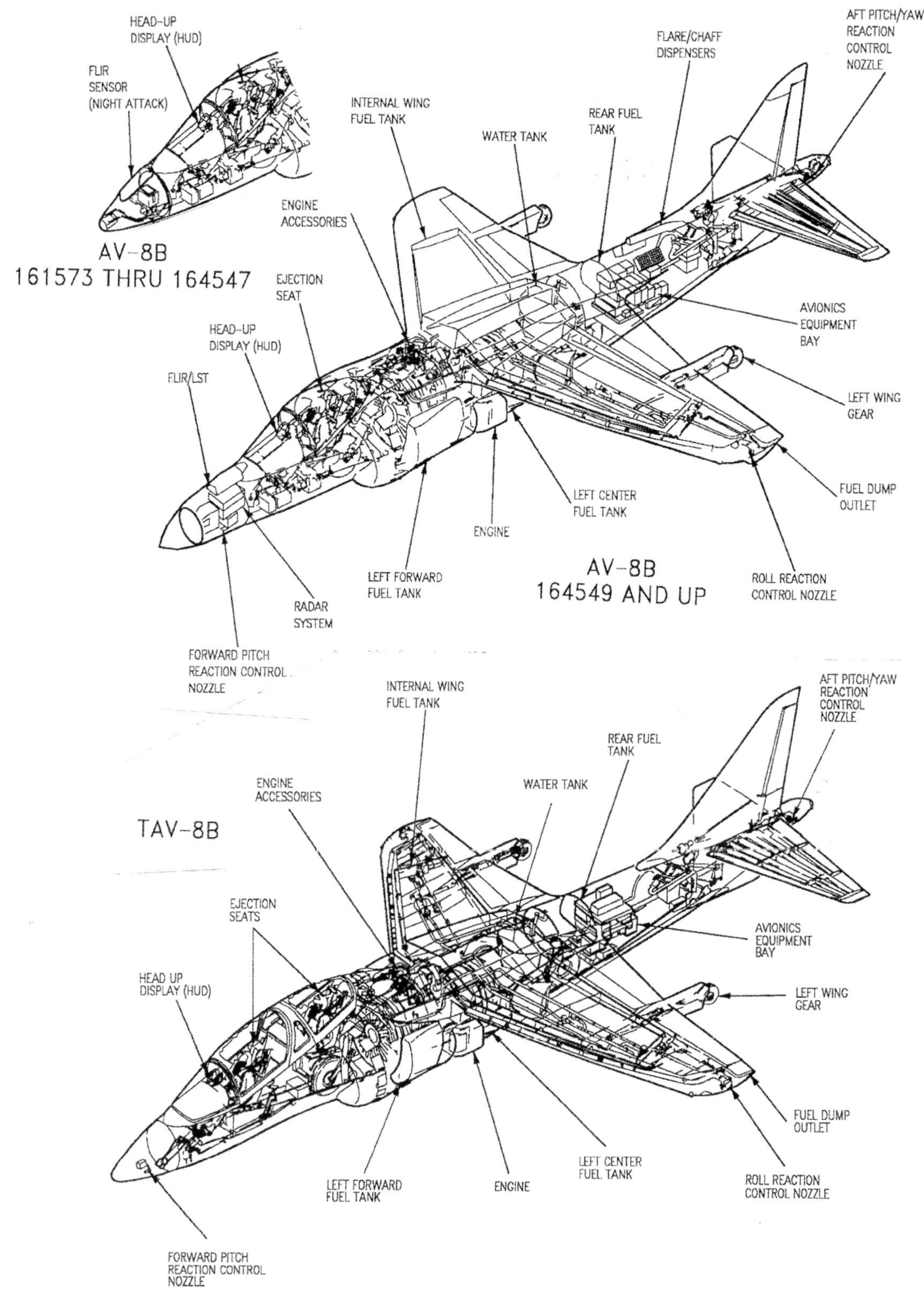

The aspect of the Harrier design that was the biggest challenge to the designer was the transition phase from vertical to forward flight. In this sequence of photos, the Harrier is demonstrating this transition by going from vertical thrust (as seen in the top photo) into forward thrust (in the bottom photo) during an air show demonstration. *Ken Neubeck*

The AV-8B Harrier is a frequent performer at air shows conducted in the US because of its unusual capabilities. Here is a Harrier from VMA-542 ("the Tigers") preparing for vertical takeoff from the runway of Stewart Airport in upstate New York, during an air show in August 2015. *Ken Neubeck*

This AV-8B Harrier from VMA-311 ("the Tomcats") is in hover mode above the crowds at the annual Oshkosh air show in 2005. *John Gourley*

The different configuration of AV-8B Harriers used by the USMC can be determined by the nose features of the aircraft. Shown here is the nose of the original AV-8B Harrier that was used by the USMC. This has the forward-looking infrared (FLIR) sensor located in the window of the nose, but no additional structures are built on top of the nose. A total of eighty-six Harriers were built in this original configuration, beginning in 1981. *John Gourley*

This is the nose of an AV-8B (NA), or night attack version. This version still has the FLIR sensor located in the window of the nose, but an additional structure containing the FLIR sensor, on top of the nose, has been added. A total of sixty-six Harriers were built in this configuration, beginning in 1987. *John Gourley*

This is the nose of an AV-8B Harrier II Plus. While the FLIR sensor is still located on top of the nose, in a rectangular box, the front of the nose has been sealed. In addition, the extended nose has the APG-65 radar installed. A total of thirty new Harriers were built in this configuration, along with seventy-two rebuilt, beginning in 1992. *John Gourley*

In addition to the nose change, additional items have been added to the forward fuselage of the Harrier II, such as the pitot probe located on the lower fuselage, as well as additional access panels for the APG-65 radar that was added to this version. *John Gourley*

The USMC ordered twenty-eight TAV-8B two-seat Harriers, used for training. This setup consists of tandem-style seating for the pilot and student. The aircraft shown here is from USMC Squadron VMAT-203, with tail code KD, and it is based out of Cherry Point, North Carolina. *John Gourley*

Side view of the TAV-8B Harrier shows the unique cockpit layout, with the student pilot in the forward cockpit and the instructor in the rear cockpit. A total of twenty-eight TAV-8B trainers were built, beginning in 1986. *John Gourley*

CHAPTER 5

UK Second-Generation Harriers

This GR5 RAF Harrier is an outdoor display for the PIMA Air & Space Museum, located in Tucson, Arizona. This GR5, serial number ZD353, was retired by the UK due to damage incurred during an electrical fire in flight on July 29, 1991, with the pilot making an emergency landing at RAF Wittering in England. This issue resulted in the GR5 fleet being grounded. This aircraft has the markings of a UK training squadron, Squadron 233, painted on it. *Pima Air & Space Museum via Chuck Stump*

Shortly after the US started the AB-8B Harrier program, the UK Ministry of Defense approved the purchase of sixty GR5 Harriers, to be built by Hawker Siddeley after the development aircraft first flew in 1985. Production would begin in 1987.

The GR5 Harrier is very similar to the AV-8B Harrier built by McDonnell Douglas, with some differences. The GR5 would have a different nose than the AV-8B since it originally was to hold all-weather reconnaissance equipment, but this did not happen. Also, the GR5 was to be outfitted with the Aden-25 gun in lieu of the GAU-12 gun used on the AV-8B. However, reliability issues were discovered and the GR5 ended up not having a gun, nor did the subsequent GR7 and GR9 models, which severely limited aspects of the close-air-support mission.

A total of forty-one new GR5 models would be built, followed by nineteen GR5A models, which had an empty nose with prewiring that would allow for equipment to be installed to make the aircraft into the GR7 model. In addition, there would be the GR9 model, which included enhanced capabilities that allowed a unified Harrier force to be developed, leading to the retirement of the FA.2 Sea Harrier. The first flight occurred in 2003.

The GR7 Harrier would see combat action in Iraq in 2003 in close-air-support roles, as well as reconnaissance missions in search for SCU missiles, later seeing combat action in Afghanistan in 2004 in close-air-support roles.

The GR9 model also saw combat action in Afghanistan in 2007 with the RAF. Both the GR7 and the GR9 would conduct intimidation, reconnaissance, and interdiction missions. All UK harriers were withdrawn from Afghanistan by June 2009, having accrued a total of 8,500 combat sorties and 22,000 flying hours.

All British Harriers would be withdrawn from RAF service by the end of 2010. The remaining seventy-two Harriers were sold to the US for spare parts in 2011. The plan is that the UK will purchase F-35B aircraft to meet the VSTOL role by 2025.

Flight Lieutenant Dave Ashley is in front of his UK GR7 Harrier during a detachment to Norway, in February 2004. *Dave Ashley*

Flight Lieutenant Dave Ashley in his GR7 Harrier over the winter landscape of Norway, in February 2004. *Dave Ashley*

An RAF GR7 Harrier lands in Aviano, Italy, on March 19, 2007, during a refueling stop. This model of Harrier would see war action in both Iraq and Afghanistan. *USAF photo by SSgt. Bethann Gaporaletti*

Flight Lieutenant Dave Ashely is seen here in his GR7A Harrier during action over Afghanistan in September 2006. Ashley would fly over seventy-eight Harrier combat missions, averaging 1.5 hours per mission, for the RAF during his tour in Afghanistan. *Dave Ashley*

An RAF GR9 Harrier in flight over Afghanistan on December 12, 2008, during combat activity there. This would be the last combat action for the GR9 Harriers, since the UK Harrier fleet would be withdrawn from the theater in 2009 and subsequently retired from service in 2010. *USAF photo by SSgt. Aaron Allmon*

CHAPTER 6

USMC Harrier Details

The AV-8A/C Harrier has a nose landing gear, a main landing gear, and two wing landing gears that are located under each wingtip. The USMC AV-8A/C Harrier had a total of four hardpoints, two under each wing for weapon pylons for an external fuel tank, as seen here. *Ken Neubeck*

Side view of the nosewheel assembly shows that it is angled toward the rear of the aircraft. *Ken Neubeck*

When the AV-8B goes into hover mode during an air show, it becomes easier to see the unique structure and characteristics of the lower half of the aircraft. In this view, the landing-gear setup is visible, with the nose, main, and wing gears. With the increase in wingspan to 30 feet for the AV-8B model over the AV-8A model, an additional hardpoint has been added under each wing (a total of six hardpoints), which allow for additional weapon pylons. *Ken Neubeck*

This photo, taken from underneath an AV-8B that is flying in hover mode, shows that the main landing gear is extended from the center fuselage and that it is a dual wheel assembly. The wing landing gears are extended from the stowing structure located on the back of each wing. The wing landing gears for the B model have been moved farther inboard from the A/C model. Flaps are extended downward on each wing during this particular hover maneuver. *Ken Neubeck*

During hover mode of this AV-8B aircraft, all landing gears are extended, and the size differences between the wing landing gears can be seen in this photo. The two wing landing gears are much smaller compared to the main landing gear, located under the main fuselage, and the nose landing gear. *Ken Neubeck*

During flight, the two wing landing gears are stowed inside a structure that extends from each wing, with the wheel assembly exposed. *Ken Neubeck*

An AV-8B Harrier from VM-311 is preparing to land on USS *America*, an amphibious ship, with all landing gears extended. In this photo, the nose landing gear, the main landing gear, and the two wing landing gears can be seen. *US Navy*

An AV-8B Harrier from VM-542 is hovering with all of the landing gears stowed—the nose landing gear in the nose, the wing landing gears in the wings, and the main landing gear in the lower fuselage. Also seen in this photo are the characteristic "elephant ears," or the engine inlets located on either side of the fuselage. *Ken Neubeck*

This USMC AV-8B Harrier aircraft from VMA-542 is in hover mode with all landing gears deployed over the crowds during the New York State Air Show in August 2017. *Ken Neubeck*

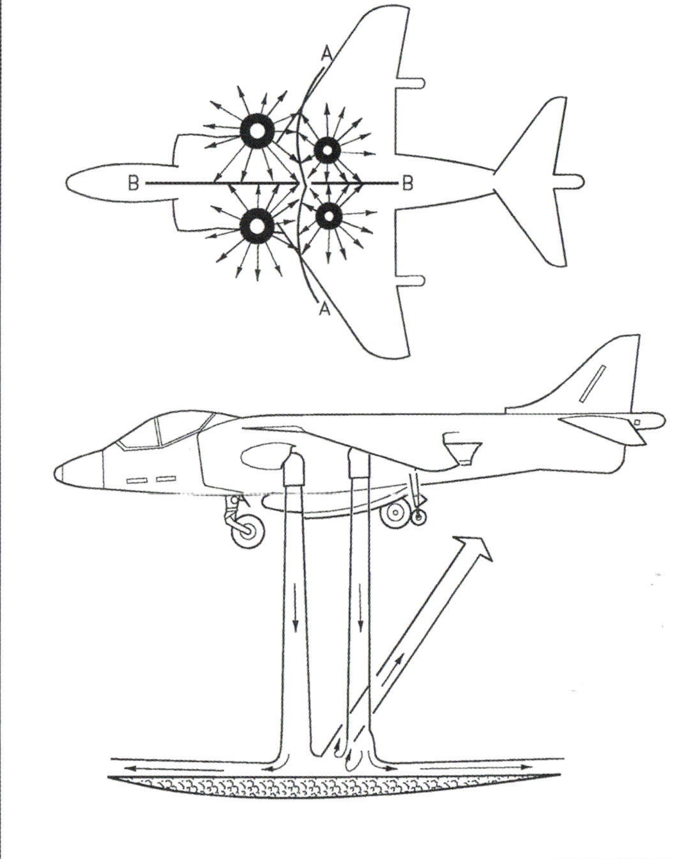

In this segment of the hover mode demonstration, all landing gears are in the "up," or stowed, position. *Ken Neubeck*

This diagram from the NAVTOPS manual shows the four engine exhaust ports of the AV-8B Harrier aircraft, which when pointed downward allows for the aircraft to hover.

Photo of the front portion of the AV-8B Harrier during hovering shows that the engine nozzle is pointed downward to provide the necessary lift for hovering. This aircraft from VMA-542 has Japanese script on its nose as an indication of being involved with joint US and Japan exercises in 2016. *Ken Neubeck*

Forward view of the AV-8B in hover mode. *USMC photo by LCpl. Dalton Swanbeck*

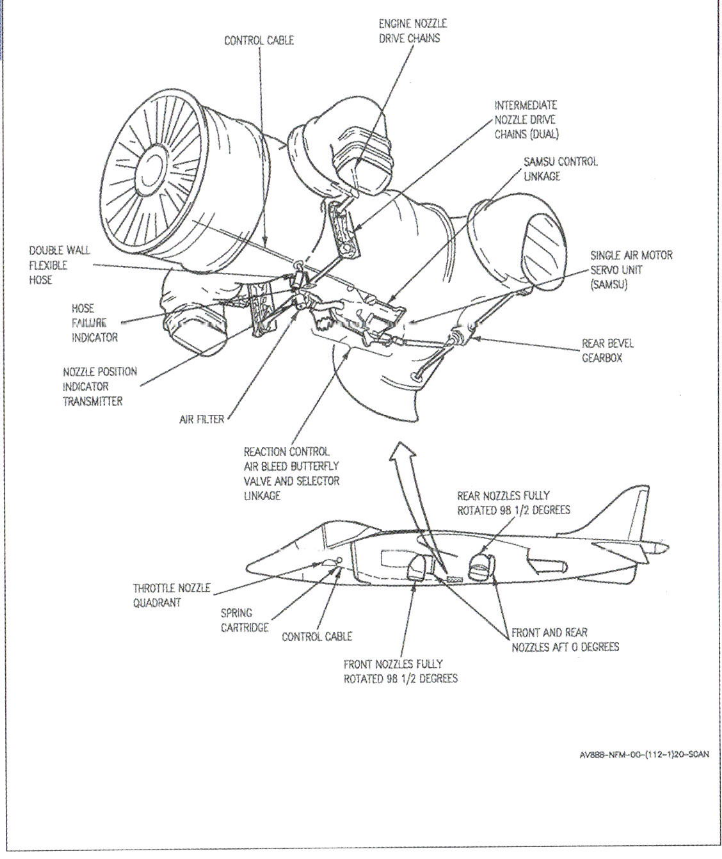

This diagram from the NAVTOPS manual shows the different features for the engine in the Harrier that allow for it to go forward as well as hover.

From this view from the rear of the Harrier, both the forward and rear exhaust nozzles can be seen. They are pointed downward for VSTOL operation. It is noted that there is some indication of corrosion on the rear nozzle, probably caused by the impact of high-temperature engine exhaust on the metal of the nozzle. *John Gourley*

This AV-8C Harrier aircraft is on display at the USS *Intrepid* Air and Space Museum, located in New York City. The Harrier has the forward nozzle pointing toward the rear, which is indicative of the forward flight mode. *Ken Neubeck*

USMC maintenance personnel from VMA-542 hoist a Pegasus 11 engine from an AV-8B Harrier aircraft for maintenance in the hangar bay of USS *Kearsarge* (LHD 3), an amphibious assault ship. *US Navy photo by MCS2c Tom Gagnier*

The inlet section consisting of the fan blades for the Pegasus 11 engine during removal by maintenance personnel can be seen here. The Pegasus turbofan engine is one of the later configurations of the Harrier engine, and it is capable of putting out 21,500 pounds of thrust. *US Navy photo by MCS2c Tom Gagnier*

A maintainer is working in the cockpit of an AV-8B Harrier in November 2014. The heads-up display (HUD) can be seen on the top of the console, along with the multifunction display located directly below it. Standard flight gauges for straight-ahead flight are located in the middle of the console. The control stick is located at the base of the console. *USMC photo by Cpl. Laura Y. Raga*

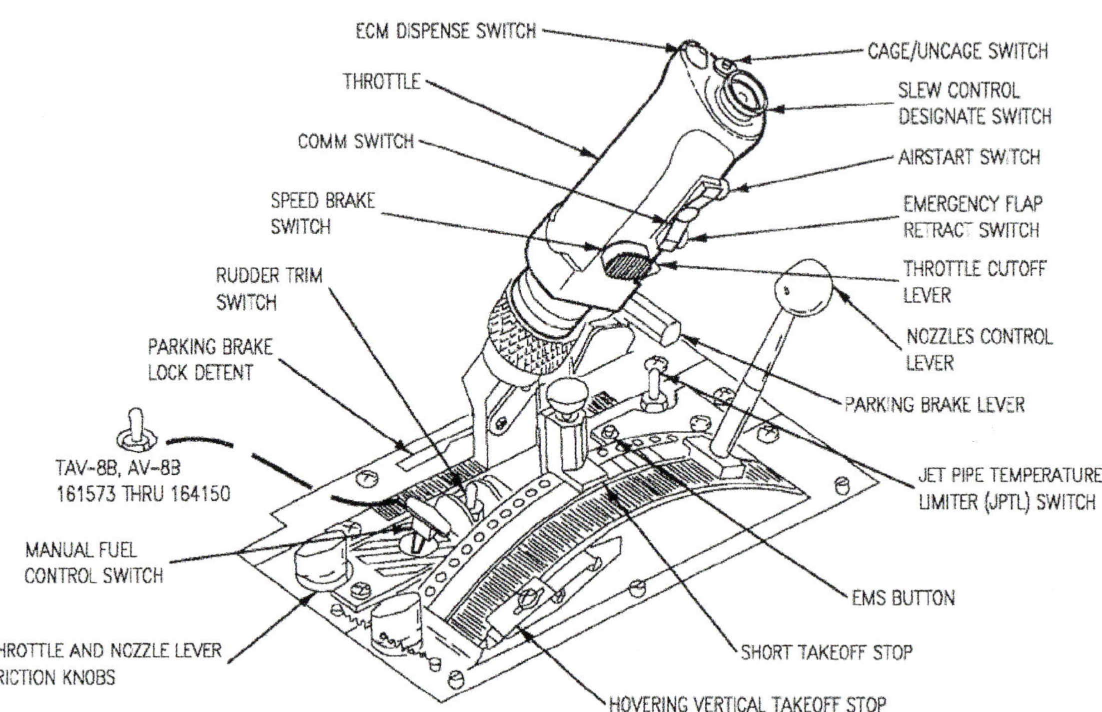

Located on the left side of the cockpit is the throttle nozzle control, which has been modified from the AV-8A version as shown in this diagram from the NAVTOPS manual.

A Marine cleans the canopy on an AV-8B Harrier on the flight deck of USS *Iwo Jima* (LHD 7), a multipurpose amphibious assault ship, during the unit-training exercise. In this photo, the main console can be seen in each aircraft, along with the heads-up display located on the top of the console. *US Navy photo by MCS 1st Class Daniel Taylor*

This pilot, Capt. Wiener, is preparing for takeoff in his AV-8B. The HUD on top of the console can be seen. The SJU-4/A ejection seat is also visible. Note the outline pattern on the top of the windshield, for the ejection seat to go through. *USMC photo by SSgt. Christopher Q. Stone*

Another photo from above the cockpit shows the pilot from VMA-223 on USS *Nassau* giving a salute as he prepares for takeoff. Note the aerial-refueling probe located on the left wing. *USMC photo by Sgt. Robert A. Sturkie*

This AV-8B Harrier is preparing for takeoff from the USMC base in Yuma, Arizona, during nighttime training. The pilot is wearing night-vision imaging system (NVIS) goggles, and the cockpit displays are illuminated in the NVIS green. *USMC photo by Cpl. Lauren Brune*

Close-up view of an AV-8B pilot shows him wearing NVIS goggles, used for nighttime flying, during operations from USS *Boxer* in October 2018. *US Navy photo by MC3 Alexander C. Kubitza*

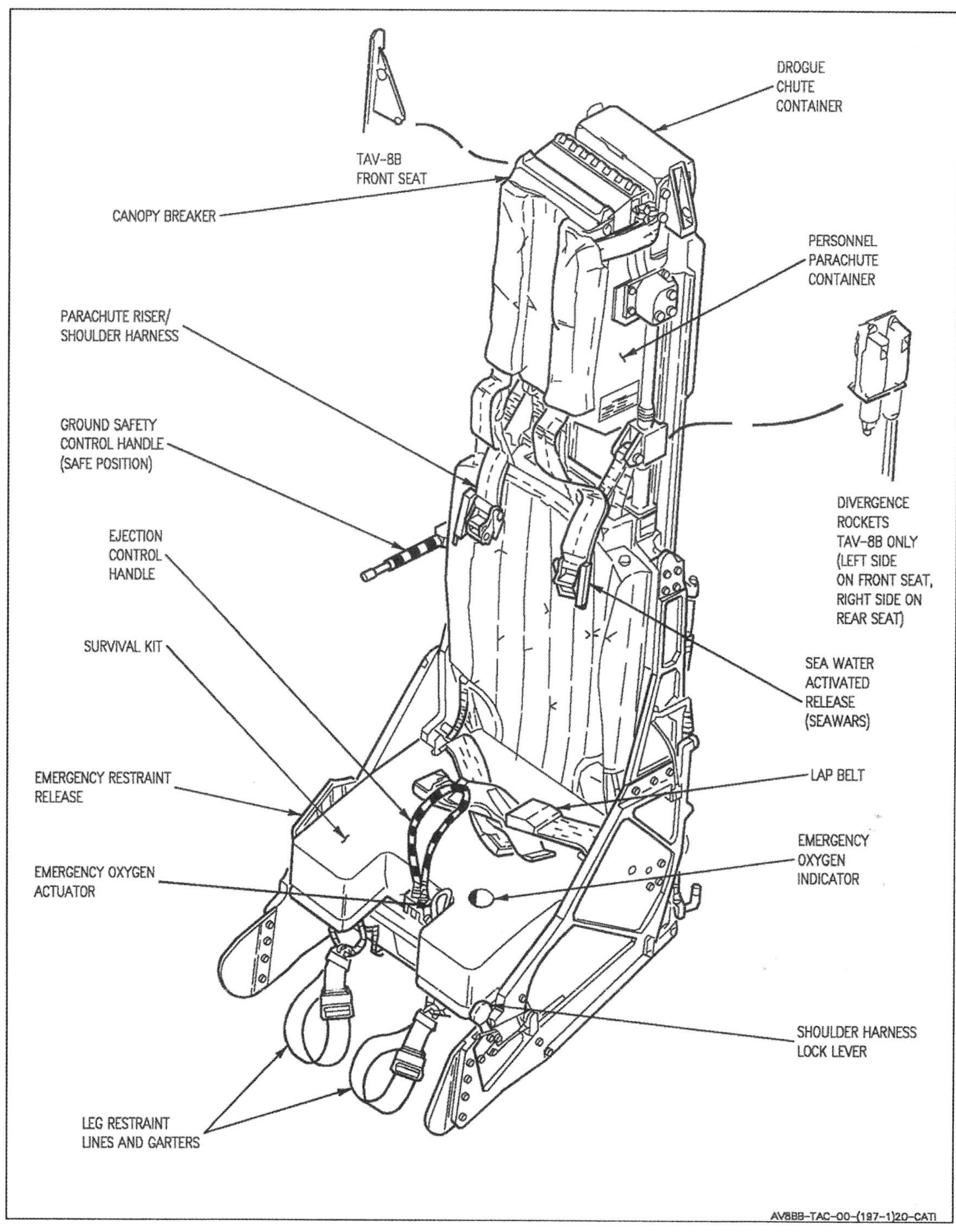

The diagram shown here from the NAVTOPS manual shows the features of the SJU-4/A ejection seat that is used on the AV-8B Harrier. The TAV-8B uses the SJU-13/A for the front seat and the SJU-14/A for the rear seat, with the difference being that the divergence rockets are located on one side, as shown in the diagram.

Maintenance crew members are busy doing comprehensive maintenance action on AV-8B Harrier aircraft in the maintenance bay of USS *Kearsarge*. The forward nose assembly has been opened to access various electronics located in the nose, including the AN/APG-65 radar, which has been removed. *USMC photo by Cpl. Andre Dakis*

Maintenance personnel are preparing to remove the multimode AN/APG-65 radar from the nose section of the AV-8B II Plus aircraft. The addition of this radar is a key feature of the AV-8B II Plus version of the Harrier. *USMC photo by LCpl. Tucker S. Wolf*

This AV-8C first-generation Harrier was equipped with two ADEN gun pods located under the center fuselage. Shown here is the left-side gun pod on this AV-8C display aircraft. *Ken Neubeck*

This is a view of the right-side gun pod located on the same AV-8C display aircraft. This particular gun proved to be very effective for the RAF Harriers when the aircraft supported UK close-air-support missions during the Falkland War, and would subsequently shoot and destroy aircraft on the ground as well as some Argentine aircraft in flight. *Ken Neubeck*

For close-air-support missions that involve ground attack, the AV-8B Harrier can be fitted with a GAU-12 gun pod, located on the left side of the center lower fuselage, and an ammo pod, located on the right side. Here is a Harrier that is equipped with the gun and ammo pods as it prepares for takeoff from USS *Kearsarge*, an amphibious assault ship, in February 2003. *US Navy photo by PH3 Angel Roman-Otero*

Here is the GAU-12 gun pod unit being loaded by maintenance personnel onto a Harrier on USS *Peleliu* in September 2008. The GAU-12 gun is also used on the AC-130 gunship. *US Navy photo by MC2 Dustin Kelley*

This is the gun pod after it was installed under the center fuselage of the Harrier. The pod weighs 270 pounds. *John Gourley*

This is a close-up of the front section of the Gatling gun pod that shows the five barrels on the face behind the opening of the front structure. The gun can fire at a slow rate of thirty rounds a second, and a high rate of seventy rounds a second. *John Gourley*

The ammunition pod contains 300 rounds of 25 mm shells, and the pod has a link that feeds the gun pod located on the other side, through a bridge channel. *John Gourley*

These 25 mm shells are being loaded by loader personnel by hand onto the track of the loading mechanism into the ammo pod. *USMC photo by LCpl. Aaron Diamant*

The first-generation AV-8A Harrier had a wingspan of 25 feet, 5 inches, which had a total of four hardpoints (two under each wing) that was capable of holding up to 5,000 pounds of bombs, external fuel tanks, or both. *John Gourley*

The second-generation AV-8B Harrier had a wingspan of 30 feet, 4 inches, which had a total of six hardpoints (three under each wing) that was capable of holding up to 9,200 pounds of bombs, external fuel tanks, or both. *USMC photo by LCpl. Cody Rowe*

Weapon-loading crew are using the bomb carrier to transport three GBU-54 JDAM bombs that have laser guidance systems attached to the nose to AV-8B Harrier on board USS *Wasp* in September 2016. *US Navy photo by MC2 Nathan Wilkes*

The AV-8B Harrier has had the incorporation of digitally controlled weapons since 2015, with the introduction of the BRU-70 Digital Integrated Triple Ejector Rack (DITER). The BRU-70 DITER can be seen here on the pylon located with two bombs, in between the external fuel cell and the outside pylon under both wings. This has expanded the Harrier's capability and effectiveness in combat action. *USAF photo by Senior Airman Tyler Woodward*

The refueling probe extends from the rear portion of the top of the left engine inlet. This is a distinctive feature of the Harrier, and for the AV-8B model it is movable via linkage that is attached to it. It can be stowed inside a track located on top of the nacelle. *John Gourley*

The refueling probe can be seen here in the lowered or stowed position. A view of the different bomb racks that are used on the Harrier's pylon and wingtip stations is seen here as well. *John Gourley*

Aerial refueling was required often when the AV-8B Harrier participated in Operation Enduring Freedom in Afghanistan. Here is a USMC AV-8B from VMA-311 undergoing aerial refueling in Helmand Province, Afghanistan, in June 2013. *USAF photo by Sgt. Gabriela Garcia*

A closer view of the aerial-refueling operation shows the refueling drogue connecting to the AV-8B probe that is extending from the top of the left engine inlet during Operation Inherent Resolve in Iraq in December 2015. *USAF photo by Senior Airman Tara Fadenrecht*

Crew members dressed in purple vests, nicknamed "grapes," are responsible for conducting ground-refueling operations on AV-8B Harrier on the deck of USS *Boxer* in January 2019. *US Navy photo by MC3 Brett Anderson*

A crew member is refueling the internal tanks of the AV-8B Harrier through the ground-refueling port located on the left side of the aircraft, below the nozzle structure. *US Navy photo by MCSN Zachary D. Behrend*

CHAPTER 7

USMC Squadrons

There have been nine different US Marine squadrons that had the AV-8 Harriers in their service. Three of these USMC squadrons started with the first-generation AV-8A and then later upgraded to the second-generation AV-8B Harrier.

There were initially four principal locations for the nine AV-8B squadrons in the US: Cherry Point, North Carolina; Opa-locka, Florida; and Yuma, Arizona. Two squadrons would be retired in the new millennium, including the closing of the base at Opa-locka due to the defense base reduction program. The training squadron, VMAT-203, has the two-seat TAV-8B aircraft on hand and is located at Cherry Point.

When USMC squadrons are deployed for operational exercises or for military action, they will typically be assigned to a USMC amphibious assault ship for the base of operations. In some military actions, they may be assigned to an air base in a country that is closest to the action, as was the case in Iraq and Afghanistan during US combat activity, and in some cases, bases in Africa.

All the current AV-8B USMC squadrons have had over thirty years of Harrier experience and have seen substantial military action during all of the US war activity during that time.

USMC Harrier Squadrons

Squadron	Nickname	Location	Tail code	Year assigned to AV-8
VMA-211	Wake Island Avengers	Yuma, AZ	CF	1990 (B)
VMA-214	Black Sheep	Yuma, AZ	WE	1989 (B)
VMA-223	Bulldogs	Cherry Point, NC	WP	1987 (B)
VMA-231	Ace of Spades	Cherry Point, NC	CG	1973 (A)
VMA-311	Tomcats	Yuma, AZ	WL	1988 (B)
VMA-331*	Doodlebugs	Opa-locka, FL	VL	1985 (B)
VMA-513*	Nightmares	Yuma, AZ	WF	1971 (A)
VMA-542	Tigers	Cherry Point, NC	WH	1972 (A)*
VMAT-203	Hawks	Cherry Point, NC	KD	1983 (B)*

Note:
* Deactivated squadrons.

VMAT-203 is the AV-8B training squadron for the USMC. It is based in Cherry Point, North Carolina, with VMA-223, VMA-231, and VMA-54. However, it can be deployed to the other USMC AV-8B base in Yuma, Arizona, such as this TAV-8B Harrier from VMAT-203 on assignment in May 2009 for training purposes. This TAV-8B aircraft is one of twenty-eight two-seater Harrier aircraft. *USMC photo by LCpl. Graham J. Benson*

A TAV-8B Harrier from VMAT-203 is in flight during training in MCAS in Beaufort, South Carolina, during Operation Angry Bird in May 2014. This squadron has the KD tail code. *USMC photo by LCpl. Austin Lewis*

An air boss is directing AV-8B Harrier from VMA-211 (Wake Island Avengers) toward forward takeoff from USS *Makin Island* in February 2014, as evidenced by the forward position of the exhaust nozzle. *US Navy photo by MC3 Kory Alsberry*

An air boss is directing AV-8B Harrier from the deck of USS *Peleliu* in March 2014. The tail code marking for this squadron is CF. *US Navy photo by MC3 Kory Alsberry*

A pair of AV-8B Harriers from VMA-214 ("Black Sheep"), with tail code WE, are preparing for operations on the deck of USS *Peleliu*, an amphibious assault ship, during carrier qualifications in August 2005. *US Navy photo by Journalist 2nd Class Zach Baddorf*

AV-8B Harriers from VMA-214 ("Black Sheep") line up for operations on the deck of USS *Essex* in February 2007. *US Navy photo by MC1c Jeremy L. Woods*

Carrier crew member moves away from an AV-8B Harrier from VMA-223 ("Bulldogs") that is conducting vertical takeoff off the deck of USS *Iwo Jima* during operations in April 2005. *USS Navy photo by Robert J. Fluegel*

An AV-8B Harrier, BuNo 164566, from VMA-223 ("Bulldogs") is on the tarmac of Patrick AFB, Florida, during a visit in January 1996 from the squadron's home base in Cherry Point, North Carolina. The Bulldog emblem is displayed on the forward fuselage, and the aircraft is carrying external fuel tanks for extended travel. *John Gourley*

An AV-8B Plus Harrier, BuNo 165354, from VMA-223 ("Bulldogs") is preparing for conventional rolling takeoff from NAS Jacksonville, Florida, in November 2002. *John Gourley*

The tail of AV-8B Harrier, BuNo 165354, shows detailed artwork depicting the bulldog and gray stripes of the squadron, along with the WP tail code. *John Gourley*

An AV-8B Harrier from VMA-231 ("Ace of Spades") is conducting a conventional forward takeoff from the deck of USS *Bataan* during exercises in the Atlantic Ocean in November 2007. *US Navy photo by MC3 Jeremy L. Grisham*

This is a top view of the same AV-8B Harrier from VMA-231 ("Ace of Spades") during its forward takeoff from the deck of USS *Bataan* during exercises in the Atlantic Ocean in November 2007. *US Navy photo by MC3 Jeremy L. Grisham*

This night-attack-version AV-8B Harrier is from VMA-311 ("the Tomcats") and is visiting Patrick AFB, Florida, in 1996. *John Gourley*

A closer view of this night-attack AV-8B Harrier, BuNo 163661, from VMA-311 shows the "Tomcat" emblem marking, with the WL tail code. *John Gourley*

The VMA-331 squadron ("Doodlebugs") was originally commissioned during World War II and operated out of Marine Corps Air Station in Opa-locka, Florida, and carried the nickname the "Doodlebugs." It was the first USMC squadron to receive an AV-8B Harrier. Here is a VMA-331 AV-8B preparing to land on the USS *Nassau* in September 1990 during Operation Desert Shield. *US Navy photo by PH1 Allen*

AV-8B Harriers from VMA-331 during a visit to Patrick AFB, Florida, in September 1991. The aircraft still features the paint scheme that was used in Desert Storm. The squadron would be deactivated in 1992 during base closure as part of defense reductions. *John Gourley*

The VMA-513 squadron was originally commissioned during World War II, in February 1944. Here is an AV-8B from VMA-513 preparing to land on USS *Peleliu* in the Pacific Ocean in April 2005. *US Navy photo by Journalist 3rd Class Zack Baddorf*

An AV-8B from VMA-513 is conducting VSTOL operations on USS *Peleliu* in the Pacific Ocean in April 2005. VMA-513, "the Nightmares," would be the first USMC squadron to receive Harrier aircraft, beginning in 1971. *US Navy photo by PM Airman Timothy Gunther*

In July 2013, USMC squadron VMA-513 would be formally decommissioned in a ceremony in Yuma, Arizona, that was headed by the squadron commander, Lt. Col. Samuel Smith, and the executive officer, Maj. Andrew Diviney, both shown saluting. *USMC photo by Sgt. William Waterstreet*

USMC color guard stand in front of two AV-8B Harriers during the decommissioning ceremony of VMA-513. The aircraft of this squadron would be dispersed to squadrons VMA-211 and VMA-311, also based in Yuma, Arizona. *USMC photo by Sgt. William Waterstreet*

An AV-8B Harrier from VMA-542 ("the Tigers") is conducting a hovering maneuver over the crowds at the New York State Air Show in August 2015. This squadron was selected for performing at a number of air shows during that year. This squadron has seen many combat-mission war theaters during its existence. *Ken Neubeck*

The tail for VMA-542 features the unique tiger stripes on the rear edge of the vertical stabilizer and the WH tail code. *John Gourley*

An AV-8B Harrier from VMA-542 is preparing for takeoff from USS *Bataan* in May 2016. "The Tigers" would see many deployments overseas in different combat theaters. *US Navy photo by MC3 Raymond Minami*

An AV-8B Harrier from VMA-542 is performing during an air show at Cherry Point, North Carolina, in May 2005. The Tigers have been performing in a limited number of air shows per year, demonstrating the hovering capabilities of the Harrier. *US Navy photo by PM2c Daniel J. McLain*

CHAPTER 8

USMC AV-8B Combat Operations

AV-8B Harriers are preparing for takeoff from the USS *Nassau* during Operation Desert Shield in September 1990. *US Navy photo by PH1 Allen*

From 1990 onward, the AV-8B Harrier would be in every major US combat activity. The following is a summary by operation.

Operation Desert Storm

With the invasion of Kuwait by Iraq, there was worldwide condemnation, and the United States was a major part of a coalition of allied forces to deploy to Saudi Arabia, initially to prevent an invasion into Saudi Arabia by Iraq in August 1990. This would be coined Operation Desert Shield by President George H. W. Bush. The US would eventually commit over 100,000 troops, along with hundreds of airplanes and tanks.

The Harrier II was the first Marine Corps tactical strike platform to arrive in the theater, and subsequently it operated from various land bases. Three squadrons had a total of sixty aircraft, and there was one six-aircraft detachment operated ashore from an expeditionary airfield, while one squadron of twenty aircraft operated from a sea platform. The aircraft initially flew training and support sorties, as well as practicing with coalition forces.

When Operation Desert Shield turned into Operation Desert Storm on January 17, 1991, many other US aircraft such as the AV-8B would be seeing combat action for the first time. The AV-8Bs operated from various bases in the region and were based on ships such as USS *Nassau* and USS *Tarawa*.

The AV-8B was first used in the operation on the morning of the first day of the war, when a call for air support came to address Iraqi artillery that was shelling Khafji and an adjacent oil refinery. The following day, USMC AV-8Bs attacked Iraqi positions in southern Kuwait. Throughout the war, AV-8Bs performed armed reconnaissance and worked in concert with coalition forces to destroy targets.

During the ground war, AV-8Bs were based less than 50 miles from the Kuwait border, making them the most forward-deployed tactical strike aircraft in theater. For the war, the AV-8B flew 3,380 sorties for a total of 4,083 flight hours, while maintaining a mission-capable rate in excess of 90 percent. Average turnaround time during the ground-war surge-rate flight operations was twenty-three minutes.

Five AV-8Bs were lost to enemy surface-to-air missiles, with two USMC pilots were killed. The AV-8B had an attrition rate of 1.5 aircraft for every 1,000 sorties flown. US Army general Norman Schwarzkopf, the head US commander, would later name the AV-8B among a number of weapons that played a crucial role in the war.

In the aftermath of the war, from August 27, 1992, until 2003, USMC AV-8Bs and other aircraft patrolled Iraqi skies in support of Operation Southern Watch. During this time, the AV-8Bs were launched from amphibious assault ships in the Persian Gulf, as well as from forward operating bases in Kuwait.

USMC AV-8B Units of Desert Storm

Squadron	Aircraft	Sorties	Flight hours	Aircraft lost	Bombs dropped (lbs.)
VMA-231	19	987	1196	1	1,692,000
VMA-311	19	1017	1230*	1	1,680,000
VMA-331	19	243	292*	2	512,000
VMA-513	6	103	123*	0	N/A
VMA-542	18	1000*	1200	1	2,000,000
Total	**81**	**3350***	**4100***	**5**	**5,700,000+**

Note:
* There were five replacement aircraft, bringing the total to eighty-six AV-8Bs used during the war. Data were compiled from various USMC sources.

USMC AV-8B Aircraft Lost during Desert Storm

Date	BuNo	Pilot	Downed by	Pilot status
January 24	163518	Capt. Michael S. Berryman	SAM	PoW
February 9	162081	Capt. Russel A. Sandorn	SAM	PoW
February 23	161573	Capt. James N. Wilborn	AAA	PoW
February 25	163190	Capt. Scott Walsh	SAM	Rescued
February 27	162740	Capt. Reginald Underwood	SAM	KIA

An AV-8B is seen here on the USS *Nassau* during Operation Desert Storm, in 1991. *US Navy*

AV-8B Harriers from VMA-513 (home base in Yuma AFB) fly in formation after refueling during Operation Desert Shield in late 1990, prior to the commencement of Operation Desert Storm. Note the green-and-gray camouflage paint scheme that is used on the aircraft. *USAF photo by SSgt. Scott Stewart*

AV-8B Harriers are on the deck of a US Navy amphibious assault ship during Operation Desert Storm in 1990. *US Navy photo by PH1 Allen*

An AV-8B Harrier at a forward base in the Middle East during Operation Desert Storm in 1990. *USAF photo by TSgt. Heimen*

AV-8B Harriers get the go-ahead to take off from a US Navy amphibious assault ship during Operation Desert Shield in September 1990, at a forward base in the Middle East. *US Navy photo by PH1 Allen*

AV-8B Harriers from VMA 331 are located on the deck of USS *Nassau*, along with UH-1N helicopters, on January 11, 1991, six days before the start of Operation Desert Storm in 1990. *USMC photo by PH1 Allen*

After the war, an AV-8B Harrier is on the flight line preparing to conduct a flyover from Andrews AFB as part of National Victory Day in June 1991. The aircraft is still in the colors that it had during Desert Storm. *Photo by LCpl. Contreras / National Archives*

The same AV-8B Harrier was later put on display in a nearby mall after the flyover during the National Victory Day event. *Photo by TSgt. Lou Comeger / National Archives*

Operation Allied Force

When Operation Allied Force began in March 1999, twelve AV-8B Harriers were deployed by the USMC from two US Navy ships, the USS *Kearsarge* and the USS *Nassau*. The AV-8B Harriers would participate in the NATO bombing campaign over the former Republic of Yugoslavia, with the USMC Harrier fleet would fly over 500 sorties, destroying significant targets in the region.

The USMC AV-8B Harriers would be supplemented during the 1999 campaign in Kosovo by RAF Harrier GR7s being deployed in the region. At the beginning of 1999, eight Harriers deployed to a base in Italy to support the Kosovo Verification Mission. This force was increased to twelve Harriers in late March. These GR7 Harriers dropped either cluster bombs, gravity bombs, or precision guided weapons. In one mission, RAF Harriers conducted cluster bomb attack on munitions storage site in Kosovo, on April 18, 1999.

Italian AV-8Bs were used for the first time in combat missions when they were deployed from the Italian aircraft carrier, *Giuseppe Garibaldi* during Operation Allied Force. Italian AV-8B aircraft conducted more than sixty sorties during the war with attacks on the Yugoslav army and paramilitary forces as well as bombing the country's infrastructure with conventional and laser-guided bombs.

No aircraft were lost during the actual combat phase of the campaign, but a USMC Harrier would crash into the Adriatic Sea during a training mission, with the pilot rescued. Combat action would cease in June 1999.

VMM-266 AV-8B Harrier preparing to land on the deck of USS *Nassau* during Operation Allied Force, in April 1999. *US Navy photo by PM1C Richard Rosser*

Six AV-8B Harriers were assigned to helicopter squadron VMM-266 on USS *Nassau* during Operation Allied Force and were marked with tail code ES in April 1999. The Harrier completed thirty-four combat sorties, accruing 65.3 flight hours. AV-8B Harrier is seen here landing after completing a mission on April 14, 1999. *US Navy photo by PM1c Richard Rosser*

Operation Enduring Freedom: Afghanistan

A total of six different USMC squadrons would participate at different times in Afghanistan, during America's longest war.

The first USMC squadron to fly over Afghanistan was VMA-311, in November 2001. Initial deployment of AV-8B Harriers were accomplished by US Navy ships. Harrier "carriers" during this initial stage included USS *Bonhomme Richard*, USS *Bataan*, and USS *Peleliu*. As the war continued on, AV-8B Harriers were deployed from land bases in Kandahar and Bagram, and later at a USMC base known as Camp Bastion, located in Helmand Province.

Deployments were typically six months, with some lasting as much as a year. One USMC squadron, VMA-513, would have a group of six aircraft that were stationed at a forward base from October 2002 through September 2003. These six aircraft amassed 1,250 sorties that encompassed 3,784 flight hours during this one-year period, with over 1,800 flight hours occurring at night through the use of the new Litening II targeting pod. The squadron provided close air support, armed reconnaissance, and combat escort as part of its duties.

There was no loss of AV-8B Harriers during the actual conducting of missions; however, a Taliban raid on Camp Bastion in September 2012, where Harriers were stationed, saw the loss of six AV-8B Harriers and two other Harriers severely damaged.

One thing that was discovered and found to be a limiting factor for AV-8B Harriers in Afghanistan was when the aircraft was based in Bagram, where the 5,000-foot altitude precluded the use of vertical takeoffs. Basing at this location did improve the ability to reach combat action deep into the country, but the VSTOL capability was not needed.

By 2018, AV-8B operations in Afghanistan had wound down, and future actions will be taken over by the F-35B aircraft slated to be introduced into USMC squadrons.

A refueling crew works on refueling AV-8B Harriers from VMA-223 ("Bulldogs") on the deck of USS *Bataan* in January 2002 in support of Operation Enduring Freedom. This squadron would have the special tail code of YM, signifying the HMM-365. *US Navy photo by PH3 John Taucher*

An AV-8B Harrier from VMA-223 ("Bulldogs") is taking off from USS *Bonhomme Richard* in January 2002, in support of Operation Enduring Freedom. *USMC photo by Sgt. Nathan Ferbert*

AV-8B Harriers from VMA-223 share the deck with USMC helicopters on USS *Kearsarge* during Operation Enduring Freedom in February 2003. *US Navy photo by PH2 Alicia Tasz*

An AV-8B Harrier from VMA-542 ("the Tigers") takes off from USS *Bataan* while in the Arabian Sea in March 2003, in support of Operation Enduring Freedom. *US Navy photo by PM 1st Class Jimmy D. Lee*

Because of the immense size of Afghanistan, aerial refueling is a common task for AV-8B Harriers flying there. An AV-8B Harrier from VMA-311 is being refueled over the Helmand Province region in June 2013. *USAF photo by Sgt. Gabriela Garcia*

AV-8B Harriers would be assigned to three main land bases during Operation Enduring Freedom. This AV-8B Harrier, from VMA-211, is at one of these bases, Camp Bastion in Helmand Province, and is going through a wing change on September 2, 2012. Unfortunately, twelve days later, on the night of September 14, the camp was attacked by Taliban invaders and there was loss of life along with the destruction of this aircraft and others. *USMC photo by Sgt. Keonaona C. Paulo*

On September 19, 2012, a memorial service was held by the US Marines at Camp Bastion in remembrance of Lt. Col. Christopher K. Raible, commander of VMA-211, who was killed during the Taliban attack. *USMC photo by Sgt. Keonaona C. Paulo*

Operation Iraqi Freedom and Subsequent Operations in Iraq

In March 2003, the US conducted attacks against the regime of Saddam Hussein in Iraq. The AV-8B Harrier was a key aircraft deployed to the region.

A total of seventy-six AV-8B Harriers were deployed to the region in early 2003 from six different USMC squadrons: VMA-211, VMA-214, VMA-223, VMA-231, VMA-311, and VMA 542. Harriers were deployed from land bases such as Al Jaber Air Base in Kuwait, where sixteen Harriers were based (from VMA-214 and VMA-231), with the balance of the Harrier fleet based from US Navy amphibious assault ships deployed to the Persian Gulf area: USS *Bataan*, USS *Bonhomme Richard*, USS *Kearsarge*, USS *Nassau*, and USS *Tarawa* as part of Force 51 seven-ship force.

During the first month of combat from March 19 to March 31, 2003, the Harrier saw significant action, with 951 combat sorties over the thirteen-day period. The bulk of major US combat activity was over by May 1, 2003, with the USMC estimating that the Harriers completed approximately 2,000 combat sorties, accruing 3,000 flight hours. The average of 1.6 hours per sortie indicates the limits of how far the Harriers traveled into Iraq. No USMC AV-8B Harriers were lost during Operation Iraqi Freedom.

There were changes this time around with this war compared to Operation Desert Storm in 1991. For this war, the AV-8B Harriers used precision-guided weapons, compared to "dumb" bombs used in 1991. There were challenges in supporting Harriers on land bases, especially with regard to fuel and weapons during the war.

Some accomplishments by individual squadrons during Operation Iraqi Freedom included VMA-542 flying 600 sorties and 1,000 combat hours from USS *Bataan*, including missions as far north as Tikrit, 400 miles away from the ship's location. A total of 170,000 pounds of ordnance was dropped by the squadron.

After the initial success of Operation Iraqi Freedom, activity would subside, but insurgent activity in Iraq would result in US forces returning to Iraq in subsequent years, in particular to deal with insurgents and later with ISIS as part of Operation Inherent Resolve.

Land base assignments would change in the ensuing years, with ten Harriers from VMA-214 being assigned to Al Asad in Iraq along with six Harriers from VMA-513 eventually being deployed to Iraq in 2006. To date, there has been no loss of Harriers in Iraq since 2003.

An AV-8B Harrier from VMA-542 is preparing for takeoff from USS *Bataan* in late February 2003, prior to the start of combat activity in Operation Iraqi Freedom. Having been a major participant in Desert Storm in 1991, this USMC squadron would see five more deployments in Iraq from 2003 through 2008, including a six-month deployment beginning in May 2004; it flew 2,171 sorties and 3,952 hours, with as many as twenty-two AV-8B aircraft assigned to the squadron. *US Navy photo by PH3 (AW) John Taucher*

This is USS *Bonhomme Richard* (LHD 6), an amphibious assault ship, on its way to the Persian Gulf in January 2003, in order to participate in Operation Iraqi Freedom. A total of thirteen AV-8B Harriers from USMC squadrons VMA-211 and VMA-311 can be seen on the deck of the ship. *US Navy photo by PM2c Jennifer Swader*

An AV-8B Harrier from VMA-311 ("Tomcats") is conducting a vertical landing onto the deck of USS *Bonhomme Richard* on March 21, 2003. During this period of the war, the "Tomcats" flew over 550 sorties while dropping 77 tons of precision ordnance, destroying or neutralizing 132 Iraqi targets. USS *Nassau* was involved both in Operation Iraqi Freedom and Operation Enduring Freedom during this particular voyage. *US Navy photo by PMR Staci Bitzer*

A Harrier pilot is on standby while another Harrier is making a vertical landing on USS *Bonhomme Richard* during Operation Iraqi Freedom on March 23, 2003. *US Navy photo by PM3rd Chris Reynolds*

One of the land-based locations that the AV-8B was deployed to was Al Asad Air Base in Kuwait, beginning in March 2003, which was used in subsequent years during US activity in Iraq. Here is an AV-8B Harrier from VMA-223 preparing for takeoff in January 2006. *USMC photo by Cpl Micah Snead*

USS *Tarawa* (LHA1) is underway from its port in San Diego, California, on a trip to the Persian Gulf in February 2003 to participate in Operation Iraqi Freedom. The ship is part of 15th MEU, which contained a six-aircraft Harrier detachment from VMA-311 to supplement the helicopters assigned to the ship, with Harriers destroying Iraqi ground targets during the war. *US Navy photo by PM3rd Chris Reynolds*

In February 2003, USS *Bataan* maneuvers its way through an eighteen-hour transit of the Suez Canal on deployment in support of Operation Iraqi Freedom. Seen on deck are AV-8B Harriers and a US Navy helicopter for this deployment. *US Navy photo by PM Airman Latrice Ames*

Operations Odyssey Dawn and Odyssey Lightning

The AV-8B would make a number of combat appearances in Libya. The first time was in March 2011 during Operation Odyssey Dawn, when US forces were brought into the region to combat troops loyal to Qadhafi. AV-8B Harriers from VMA-542 ("Tigers") were assigned to USS *Kearsarge* in the Mediterranean Sea, and on March 20, 2011, these Harriers were launched from USS *Kearsarge* in enforcing the UN no-fly zone over Libya. They carried out airstrikes on Sirte on April 5, 2011. Multiple AV-8B Harriers were involved in the defense of a downed F-15E pilot, attacking approaching Libyans prior to the pilot's extraction by an MV-22 Osprey. From March through early April, VMA-542 flew eighty-six combat sorties, accruing 220 hours and destroying seventy-two targets, with most of these missions occurring at night. After this major period of combat, the Harriers were moved to Sigonella, Italy, during April, where they would be on alert for additional surveillance operations. The squadron returned to the US in May 2011, after accruing over 1,000 hours of flight during Operation Odyssey Dawn.

The region would flare up again in June 2016 with the invasion of ISIS forces into Libya. This time, AV-8B Harriers from VMA-542, operating from USS *Wasp*, attacked ISIS targets at the request of the Libyan government as part of Operation Odyssey Lightning.

Beginning on August 1, 2016, the US launched a mix of manned and unmanned air strikes on ISIS targets near Sirte, Libya, using Harriers from USS *Wasp*.

A major advantage that the Harrier had in the role of close-air-support operations was that it could be launched from amphibious assault ships instead of land-based airbases in the region, such as locations in Sicily, part of Italy, where USAF aircraft such as the A-10 were launched from. By having ships such as USS *Wasp* stationed in the Mediterranean Sea near Libya, the AV-8B Harriers were close enough to respond quickly to different threats that occurred in Libya.

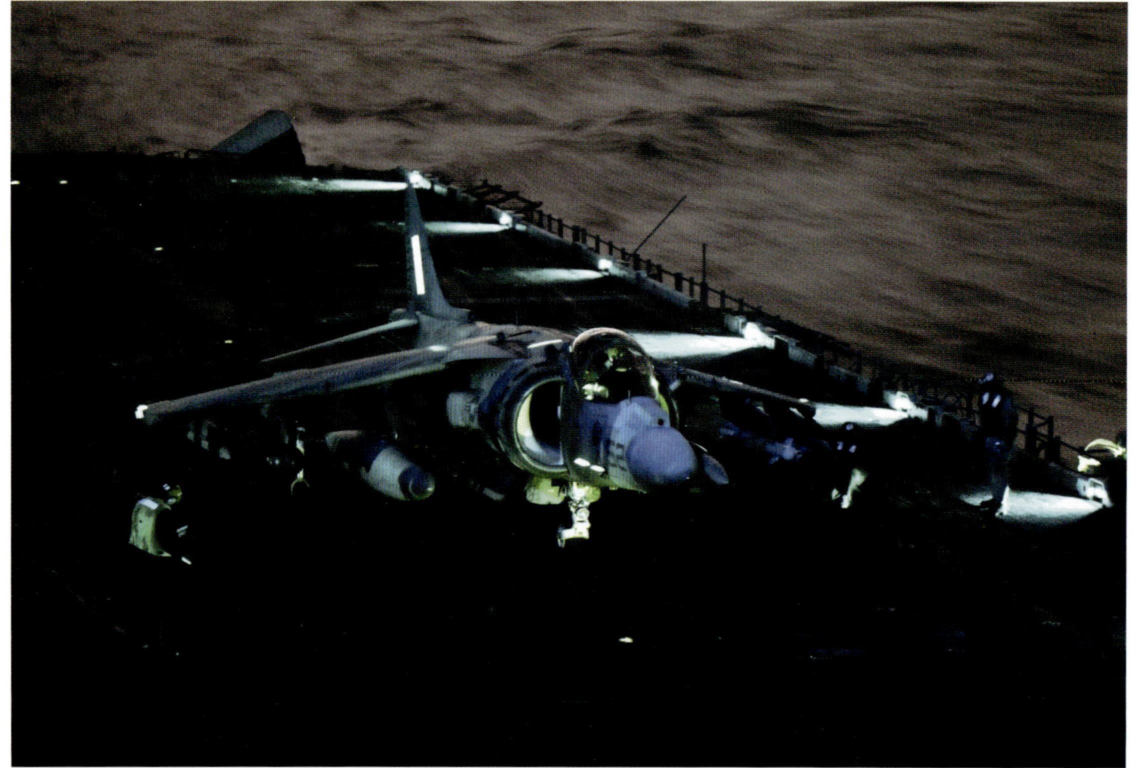

AV-8B Harriers from VMA-542 have returned to USS *Kearsarge* for ammunition resupply and refueling during raids in Libya on March 21, 2011, as part of Operation Odyssey Dawn. *USMC photo by Lance Corporal Michael S. Lockett*

Five years later, the AV-8B Harriers from VMA 542 would return to the Mediterranean Sea by Libya, this time to support Operation Odyssey Lightning in attacks on ISIS forces. AV-8B Harrier takes off from USS *Wasp* on April 8, 2016, in support of operations there, as part of Operation Odyssey Dawn. *US Navy photo by PO1c Eric S. Garst*

Operations in Libya would continue throughout the balance of 2016. Here is an AV-8B Harrier from VMA 542 ("Tigers") in support of the 22nd MEU, taking off under the direction of the air boss in the yellow vest from USS *Wasp* on December 5, 2016. The Harrier is on its way to Sirte, to attack ISIS forces there. Combat would end on December 6 with the last of ISIS forces defeated. *US Navy photo by PO2c Nathan Wilkes*

CHAPTER 9

Foreign Harriers

Summary of Foreign Harriers (outside the US and UK)

Country	First-generation Harrier	No.	Second-generation Harrier	No.
India	FRS.51	6	AV-8B II+	16
	T-60	2	TAV-8B	2
Italy		—	AV-8B II+	16
			TAV-8B	2
Spain	AV-8S	10	EAV-8B	20
	TAV-8S	2	TAV-8B	1
Thailand	AV-8A (AV-8S) (from Spain)	7		
	TAV-8A (from Spain)	2		

The Harrier was used by other naval aviation forces outside the US and the UK. First-generation Harriers were initially transferred from the UK to two countries: India and Spain. Later on, Spain would transfer its AV-8S-designated Harriers to Thailand, where they would see a few years of service.

Second-generation Harriers (AV-8B) were sold to India, Italy, and Spain, with the latter being designated EAV-8B. None of the Harriers from these countries would see any combat action in Afghanistan or Iraq.

One of ten AV-8S Spanish Matador aircraft in flight in June 1988 over the Spanish aircraft carrier *Dedalo*. *US Navy photo by Lt. Cmdr. John Leenhouts*

An EAV-8B Spanish Harrier is in the process of vertical takeoff from the Spanish aircraft carrier *Principe de Asturias* in February 2007, during joint US and Spanish NATO exercises in the Balearic Sea. Spain would receive twenty EAV-8B Harriers. *US Navy photo by MCS Leonardo Carrillo*

A Spanish AV-8B Harrier is undergoing final flight checks prior to takeoff from USS *Bataan* in June 2011 during joint US and Spain exercises in the Atlantic Ocean off the coast of Spain. *US Navy photo by MC2c Julio Rivera*

AV-8 Harrier accidents were not limited just to the US and the UK. This is the wreckage of a AV-8S Spanish Harrier, serial number VA.1-11, that went off the runway due to crosswinds at the Rota Air Base in July 1986. The pilot was able to eject safely. *US Navy photo by PH2 David J. Cummings*

Sailors work around an Indian navy FRS.51 Sea Harrier on the Indian aircraft carrier INS *Viraat* in September 2007, during joint US and Indian operations in the Indian Ocean. This is a first-generation Harrier in foreign service. *US Navy photo by MC2c Dustin Q. Diaz*

An Indian navy FRS.51 Sea Harrier on the Indian aircraft carrier INS *Viraat* in September 2007 prepares for takeoff. This is one of six Sea Harriers in the Indian navy inventory. The Indian navy would later procure sixteen AV-8B Harriers. *US Navy photo by MC2c Dustin Q. Diaz*

Sailors remove chocks from an Italian AV-8B Harrier on board the deck of USS *Kearsarge* during joint US and Italian operations in October 2015 in the Mediterranean Sea. Italy has sixteen AV-8B Harriers in its inventory. *US Navy photo by MCSA Ryre Arciaga*

An AV-8B Harrier from the Italian naval squadron is preparing for takeoff from the deck of USS *Bataan* during joint US and Italian operations in September 2017 in the Mediterranean Sea. *US Navy photo by MC3c Evan Thompson*

Ten of the AV-8A first-generation Harriers were transferred from Spain to the Royal Thai Navy in Thailand during the 1990s, and the aircraft would operate for only a few years there. Thus, only a few photos of the AV-8 while in Royal Thai Navy service exist, such as this photo of a single AV-8A Harrier on the deck of Thailand's *Chakri Naruebet*, an aircraft carrier, in April 2001 in the South China Sea. *US Navy photo by PH3 Alex C. Witte*

This is another view of *Chakri Naruebeet* on the same day as the top photo. The single AV-8A Harrier is in the middle of the deck, along with three SH-70 Seahawk helicopters. The setup used on this ship is similar to that used on US Navy amphibious assault ships, where both Harriers and helicopters are used. *US Navy photo by PH3 Alex C. Witte*

CHAPTER 10

Legacy of the Harrier Jump Jet

The F-35B Lightning II is the heir apparent to the jump jet role for the US Navy and US Marines. This is a F-35B aircraft in hover mode during sea trials with VMM-265 off USS *America*, an amphibious assault ship, in the South China Sea in April 2020. *USMC photo by Sgt. Audrey M. C. Rampton*

The USMC AV-8B Harrier was a major step in proving the effectiveness of VSTOL aircraft in military service. The Harrier proved its worth in the close-air-support role for the USMC, and it proved to be an additional choice for the role besides the USAF A-10 Warthog, which is the primary workhorse for the close-air-support role.

Perhaps the highlight of the Harrier's service career was the performance of the UK GR.3 Harrier and FRS.1 Sea Harrier during the 1983 Falklands War, where the aircraft shot down enemy aircraft and was effective in destroying ground targets. The results were dramatic in this war, and the USMC Harriers would prove to be effective in US combat activity action as well, being recognized as a key weapons system in Operation Desert Storm.

The Harrier showed that its versatility in where it could be based was significant, since it could be deployed both from land bases and US Navy ships. The downside, however, was that there was a significant amount of logistic support required for the land-based Harriers in terms of men and equipment.

There will still be a need for a VSTOL aircraft in the future for the US, since US Navy amphibious assault ships, known as "Harrier Carriers," will still be employed to carry helicopters and VSTOL aircraft around the world as needed, given that they can be deployed in a quicker manner than conventional aircraft carriers. Indeed, the Harrier saw action in parts of Africa and Asia during its career in conjunction with smaller yet still-important military action by the US military.

The replacement for the AV-8B Harrier is the F-35B Lightning II, with the AV-8B originally supposed to be phased out by 2020. However, this deadline was extended for two reasons: delays in the F-35B program, and the increased wear-out of legacy US Navy F/A-18 Hornets, which has been occurring at a higher rate than expected.

Indeed, the VSTOL F-35B version may preclude the need for the F-35C Navy version if new aircraft carrier configurations are considered, such as where the arresting cable is no longer needed for catching aircraft when they land. This would be a change in paradigm and may take decades to accomplish.

The F-35B will improve upon the Harrier, with over 40,000 pounds of thrust compared to 23,500 pounds by the AV-8B Harrier II. The F-35B produces much less exhaust than the Harrier and is thus safer to the personnel on the flight deck.

There are no new plans to procure any more AV-8B Harriers, and the plan is for the new F-35B aircraft to eventually take over the role of the AV-8B, although the Harrier continues in service with the help of spare parts from discontinued UK Harriers.

An AV-8B Harrier with VMM-163 sits on the deck of USS *Boxer* in June 2019, at night during a special photo op. *USMC photo by LCpl. Dalton S. Swanbeck*

An AV-8B Harrier is in hover mode during an air show in upstate New York in August 2015. It is one of the more unusual aircraft to perform at air shows conducted in the US. *Ken Neubeck*

This unique photo taken at night shows an AV-8B Harrier on the deck of USS *Boxer* during deployment in the Pacific Ocean in May 2019. *USMC photo by LCpl. Dalton Swanbeck*

The use of VSTOL aircraft such as the AV-8B Harrier on US Navy amphibious assault ships such as USS *Tarawa*, shown here, in lieu of aircraft carriers has given the US Navy a flexibility that will be continued with the new F-35B aircraft for many years. *US Navy photo by MSC Seaman Jon Husman*